Tales of Survival:
Domestic Violence

Copyright© 2017 Asoral Publishing

All rights reserved, including the right to reproduce this book or portions thereof in any form whatsoever. Including photocopying, recording, or by any information storage and retrieval system, without permission in writing from the copyright owner.

ISBN-13: 978-0-9970087-6-0
ISBN-10: 0-9970087-6-8

Some names and identifying details have been changed to protect the privacy of individuals. We have tried to recreate events, locales and conversations from memories of them. We may have changed some identifying characteristics and details such as physical properties, occupations and places of residence.

Cover design Copyright © 2017 by Asoral
Book design and production by LJ Thomas
Editing by LJ Thomas
www.purelypositiveshow.com
purelypositiveshow@gmail.com

Dedication

This book is dedicated to the survivors, silent sufferers, punishers and advocates who are touched by this plague. To the children who have lived with this situation and felt helpless. To the brothers, friends, fathers and others who did not know this was happening to someone loved by them. To the mothers, sisters, friends and acquaintances who were not aware of this plague in relation to a loved one. Please help stem the tide of domestic violence/abuse.

Acknowledgements

Thank you to all of the contributors of this book. I could not have done it without your courage. Thank you to the people who encouraged me to put this book together and those who helped to make it possible. A **Special Thank You** to the courageous survivors whose story is told within these pages. Selena, thank you for the work you do to bring awareness to domestic abuse. Thank you to both Sandras for your poetic expressions. Herman, you have penned awesome words of encouragement for this project.

Naturally, I thank my heavenly father for giving me the courage and tools to do this book. This is my way of speaking out. Thank you to the readers and those who have helped and encouraged me along this journey. Many of you do not even know what you did to help me.

Introduction

As I sat in the back of the waiting room, I watched as the man roughly grabbed the woman's arm and pulled her to a seat. Once they were seated, he leaned over and said, "Don't start. I don't wanna hear that whining from you today."

She sniffled. In reply to this he said, "Straighten up your face. Did you bring everything?"

"Yes. I think so." she answered.

"You think? You are so stupid. If I have to get up to come back down here with you, you know what's gonna happen." he threatened.

We were sitting in the waiting room for a food pantry. Immediately I thought to myself, "If you did your part, then you might not have to be here to get help." But, then I realized that he may have recently lost his job and not everyone was there to receive help. Either way, he was going to benefit." It made me angry. Since they were there for assistance, they were called before me and I watched him walk ahead of her as he barked for her to hurry up. She seemed tired and worn out. She kept her head and eyes down. Even when they stood up to go back and I smiled at her, she immediately looked away.

In the U.S.A, every nine seconds a woman is assaulted or beaten. Around the world, at least one in every three women have been beaten, coerced into sex or otherwise abused during her lifetime. Most often the abuser is a member of her family. Studies show that at least ten million children witness at least some form of domestic violence annually. These statistics focus on women, but men are affected as well. The domestic violence against men is on the rise. According to statistics, more than 830,000 men are victims of domestic violence in the USA each year. Domestic violence is a plague on society, but it is widely accepted. Why? One reason is that the things done to us by our parents which do not involve physical abuse, are accepted. The general attitude is, "It was done to me and I turned out okay" or "If it was good enough for my parents to do when raising me, then it's good enough for you." So, I ask you, when someone you love is screaming at you and belittling you, is that the same emotion you want to give the child you love with all of your heart? Have you asked the person doing this to you, if they liked it when it was done to them? As children, we endure things and then grow up and find ourselves either repeating the same behavior or enduring it again. Sadly this cycle is common.

In gathering the information for this book, I met a woman in her 50's who claimed that she never had any kind of involvement with domestic violence/abuse. We talked for a while and by the end of our conversation, she recanted that statement. She realized that the way she spoke to her children, although grown, but especially when they were growing up, was a form of domestic abuse. When I asked her why she always yelled and screamed at them she said, "My mother has done that to me all of my life. So, I assumed it was okay to treat my children that way. But, I've always been afraid of my mother and I don't want my children to be afraid of me. I don't want my grandchildren to be afraid of me, either. I have to change this. I'm expecting my first grandchild in a few months." She went on to say that now she realizes why her children do not spend time with her or barely call her. They visit their father when she is not at home and they call to speak to him all the time. She said it hurts her, but she thought it was normal since her relationship with her mother is the same. She didn't have a father in the picture so she didn't realize just how different it was. I felt sorry for her, but she said she would be making some changes.

Unfortunately, many of us live with this and rarely give it any thought. Until, I decided to do this book, I thought I had never been in a domestically abusive relationship. However, I had to finally recognize the signs and admit that I was in an abusive relationship in high school. This is common and mistakenly thought to be love.

Each day there are men and women who are suffering in silence. They aren't letting anyone know what goes on behind closed doors. Physical abuse, financial and emotional abuse is common.

But, that doesn't mean it is right and it should not be accepted.

I went to a doctor's appoint a few months back and for some reason, the receptionist and I hit it off. The second time I was there she casually mentioned that she was abused by her ex-husband. This was before I ever mentioned that I was doing a book on the subject. Domestic abuse crosses all boundaries (socioeconomic, ethnic, religious and sexual). There are many groups subject to this plague. It is worldwide and has been present for thousands of years.

There may be circumstances where there is nothing you can do, or you feel that way. Learn the signs. Learn what you can do to prevent or avoid being in this destructive kind of relationship. This book not only contains the true accounts of survivors written by them, but it also has valuable information and resources. There are encouraging words to be found within these pages as well as hope for violent situations. Men and women live with this every day and if we continue to look away, it will never stop.

Sincerely,

LJ Thomas

Table of Contents

Selena's Story	10
Visible, Invisible	32
Too Scared To Breathe	34
A History of Battery	36
Poetry: Wisdom & Encouragement	71
Types of Domestic Violence	80
Prevention	99
Resources	115
Myths	141
Against Men	148
Safety Plans	167
Safety Tips	207

This is a second edition of this book. The stories in the first part have been retold to reflect cleaner language, so they are no longer in the survivor's words. However, it is still their story. The content has not changed.

Selena's Story: A Wasted 10 Years

By Selena Walton

Asoral Publishing

A Wasted 10 Years
Selena Walton

Selena's Story
by Selena Walton

Hi my name is Selena Walton and I'm here to tell my story involving domestic violence which I endured at the hands of my ex-husband. Before I get started, I know there are a lot of women and girls out there going through the same things I've been through. They are keeping quiet about the situation while it's occurring and I'm telling you that's not good. CALL THE POLICE!! Keeping quiet is not good because the abuse will keep happening until you are dead or in prison. Yeah I know you are saying right about now that, "I have called the police on him, but he is still putting his hands on me."

The type of guys that don't care if you call the police on them are the type of guys that have a serious mental issue. You need to wake up and get out of there before it's too late. It just keeps repeating the cycle called the" Cycle of Violence". First it starts with the Abuse, then Guilt, then Excuses, then the Honeymoon stage, then the Fantasy and right back to the Abuse. Once you start reading my story you will become familiar with the cycle of violence.

Well I was 22 years old when I met my ex and he was 36. I thought I met the right man just because he was much older than I was. He was so sweet to me at first, but after dealing with him for about a month or so,

A Wasted 10 Years
Selena Walton

he started calling me names from a whore to a *&^(#$ and then some. He didn't care who was around when he would call me names. The name calling didn't stop there. One day I was over his house and he just started going off on me just because he was mad at someone else. He said, "Get the _____ out!"

I said, "What's going on?"

He said again, "Get the _____ out." I got up to leave and as I was going out the door he pushed me down the step, but I caught my balance and didn't fall. He then came outside and as I was opening my car door he punched me in the jaw and I lost my balance and fell into my car, dazed. Then I got myself together and realized that the whole side of my face was swollen and my nose was bleeding. The first thing he said was, "I'm so sorry, I don't know what got into me. I won't do that again. Please forgive me. I guess I'm in love with you."

Well of course, I believed him, thinking, "Oh man this man is in love with me that's why he's acting this way towards me." I convinced myself that he wouldn't do this if he didn't love me. The abuse still continued, at least 3 times a week if not more. He called me to come up to his house and I said, "Ok I will be there."

He said, "Now!"

A Wasted 10 Years
Selena Walton

It took me about twenty minutes to get there and when I did he was outside and said, "What took you so _____ long?"

I said, "I had to get myself together first."

He said, "F___ you _____, get the ____ out my face. I know you was ____ing some other nigga you dirty stinking whore." As I was about to pull off, he took his fist and punched my driver side window out as he yelled, "Get the ____ out my yard _____, you whore!"

I proceeded to pull off and he threw something at my car, missing it by inches. I was crying, "This is it, I'm done." He kept calling my phone and I wouldn't answer it. My heart was racing and my mind was all over the place thinking about whether I should do this or that to him, but of course nothing happened.

The next day he came to my house apologizing again saying, "I'm sorry, I won't do it again." and so forth. I accepted his apology again. Later on we moved in together and he asked me to marry him so I said "Yes."

He had gotten locked up later on for selling drugs. He said, "We can get married while I'm in jail so you can stay faithful to me."

I said, "I can be faithful without being married." He insisted we get married so I agreed. Nothing changed

A Wasted 10 Years
Selena Walton

while he was in there because he was trying to run me while he was doing his bid. It was becoming real stressful dealing with all this ____ that he wanted me to do. When I didn't do it in a timely manner he was pissed. I went to visit him on a Saturday and when he came out to sit down in the visiting hall, he stared at me and sat down.

I said, "You not going to give me a hug." In response he said, "I don't feel like it." At that point I knew something was wrong with him. I just sparked up a conversation and within seconds he started going off saying, "Get out of my _____ face _____."

I said what's wrong with you?"

He said again, "Get the ____ out my face _____." I got up and started to back away from him not turning around.

"Trifling ___ _____ _____" He was getting louder and louder and it was becoming really embarrassing to me so I finally said something right when I got to the door to exit the visiting hall. I said, "____ you to _____, I'm out here in society where you trying to get at." As soon as I said that he started coming after me, but the officers grabbed him. He lost his visiting privileges for three months which I was happy about. I didn't talk to him for about two weeks after that episode took place. He kept calling, but I didn't answer.

Asoral Publishing

A Wasted 10 Years
Selena Walton

When I finally talked to him, it was the same old stuff, "I'm sorry. I was just pissed off because I'm in here away from you and I'm afraid I'm going to lose you."

I believed what he was saying to me because he sounded so sincere. So I forgave him again saying, "I know you probably frustrated 'cause you're in there, but hey it's not the end of the world just come out and walk a straight and narrow path." When he got out of jail four years later, he didn't change any as far as selling drug, fighting me and calling me names. One of our friends was staying with me when he got out of jail and behind my back he was asking her who was I _____ when he was locked up.

She said, "Don't be asking me nothing about Selena. I'm quite sure you already asked her."

He instantly got mad at her calling her a _____ and told her, "You need to get the ____ out of here because she is just like you, a whore." I told her she didn't have to go anywhere, but she insisted. He never knew that she had told me about all of this. She moved out to avoid conflict with him. As time went on, he became more and more violent toward me. He would come home and start an argument with me which led to a fight. He came home one night and I was watching TV and he tried to accuse me of looking out the window of the apartment building and then I ran back inside.

A Wasted 10 Years
Selena Walton

I said, "What are you talking about? I was not out in the hall looking out the window." I got up off the couch and headed to the bedroom to ignore him and he followed calling me all kinds of names. I didn't say anything to him, but as I was getting into the bed, he punched me in the eye. I didn't say anything, but picked up the phone and called 911. He snatched the phone out of my hand and thought he hung it up. So we began to fight and the whole time the 911 dispatcher was on the phone hearing all the commotion. The next thing I knew the police were banging on the door. He looked out the peep hole and saw that it was the police. He said "Oh No! I'm going to jail." He wouldn't open the door.

The police was still banging saying, "Open up or we are going to kick the door down! We heard a women screaming in there!" So he opened the door and at that time I was in the bathroom. They came charging in looking for me and when they spotted me in the bathroom looking in the mirror and saw that my eye was swollen, they asked me did he do that to me. I said yes and they placed him under arrest. I was relieved because I knew that he wasn't going to hit me anymore 'cause he knew now that I was capable of calling the police. I felt bad because I called the police on him after he was gone.

When he came home after four hours, he was mad and didn't say anything to me and slept in the other room. He was on the phone and saying to somebody that if I loved him I wouldn't have called the police on him. I

A Wasted 10 Years
Selena Walton

told him, "I wasn't wrong for calling the police on you and if you loved me you wouldn't be hitting on me." After saying that he said, "____ you _____. You whore. You ain't ____."

    I got into my car and left. He called me five minutes later saying, "I'm sorry. I love you so much. Come on home so we can talk." I went back home and he just wanted to have sex, but I refused and he got mad all over again and you already know what kind of words he said to me. He left slamming the door and I didn't see him until the next day. He didn't communicate with me for about two weeks. As time went on the abuse was still occurring with me missing a lot of days from work because of black eyes and busted lips. One day I went to get my hair done and he kept calling my phone rushing me to hurry up and get home. He felt that it was taking way to long and he was getting real mad so my hairdresser noticed what the phone call was about and he hurried up to get me out of there.

    When I got home he wanted to accuse me of cheating, saying, "It don't take that long to get your hair done, I know you was out _____ somebody else, pull your pants down so I can check."

    I said, "You must be crazy I'm not doing that, you must don't trust me." and he said, "No _____ I don't trust you with all those _____ that been up in you while I was in jail."

A Wasted 10 Years
Selena Walton

  I said, "Whatever." Then he pushed me and looked at me with hate in his eyes and then he left. Later when he got back, I was getting myself dressed to go out with my friends to a party. He said, "You look like some ____. You think you look good but you don't. You need to take a second look in the mirror because you think you cute, but you not." then he laughed, but I just ignored him. Then he said, "You not going anywhere." But I continued to get dressed not saying a word and he walked out and the next minute he was throwing a hot cup of Theraflu in my hair while I was putting my shoes on. I jumped up in pain and said, "Why in the ____ you do that?"

  He looked at me like he wanted to kill me and said, "____ you ____, if you don't like it do something about it." I just shook my head and went into the bathroom to wash my hair not saying a word because deep down inside I was scared because I felt that he was going to kill me 'cause of the look in his eyes. My scalp was so sore 'cause of the hot sticky liquid. I had to keep putting Vaseline in my scalp for a week so I wouldn't get any blisters and couldn't even get my hair done for a while until my scalp was healed.

  The abuse didn't stop there. We moved to another area and things got even worse. It got to the point that I would sleep with my clothes on when he wasn't home because I didn't know what was going to happen when he got there. One night he came home and

A Wasted 10 Years
Selena Walton

pulled the cover off me and said, "Get the ___ out ___!" and he immediately started fighting me. He punched me in my mouth, splitting my top lip wide open, but he didn't care. I put a wet wash cloth over my mouth and drove myself to the hospital.

When I got there the nurse asked me what happened and I said, "I got in a fight with some girls."

She asked me, "Do you want me to call the police?"

I said, "No I'm cool, I will handle it myself." That day I ended up getting six stitches on the outside of my lip and three stitches in the inside, but I went right back home 'cause he claimed that it wasn't going to happen again. I missed almost two weeks of work so no one could see my injuries. When I returned to work, my co-workers were asking what happened to my lip, but of course I made up a story that I got in a car accident and my mouth hit the steering wheel. My supervisor knew what really happened because I told her the truth from the start. We were really good friends and she told me to leave him before he kills me and if I didn't have a place to go that I could come stay with her as long as I needed, but I refused her offer.

Time passed by and I found out I was pregnant and I tell you I was not happy about it at all. I was so miserable, not because I was pregnant, but who I was pregnant by. Even though I was pregnant, it didn't stop

A Wasted 10 Years
Selena Walton

the abuse. He would call me names and say I wasn't pregnant by him and that it was probably someone I worked with. I would ignore him and one day he pushed me so hard that I fell backwards and I was inches away from hitting my head on the corner of the bed frame. He didn't care because the only thing he said was, "_____you need to find out who your baby daddy is 'cause I'm not your child's father. You are a whore and a slut, _____! You think I'm stupid enough to fall for that _____." He was laughing.

The verbal abuse continued. So one day I decided that I didn't want a child by this man because when I left him I didn't want any strings attached. So I called on my supervisor/ friend and asked if I made an appointment to get an abortion would she take me. She was all for it because she knew what was going on. After I got it done, I knew it was for the best. He didn't even know what I had done. Like he cared, later that day the name calling started up again, as usual. I was lying down and he said, "Get your ___ up. Don't be lying in bed now when you was out all day laid up _____ another _____."

I said, "Whatever." and then he pulled the cover off me.

I said, "Would you please leave me alone? I didn't say anything to you and you always trying to start a fight with me all the time and for the record I had a

A Wasted 10 Years
Selena Walton

miscarriage today." He just looked at me without saying a word and then walked off.

Days went by and he was being Mr. Nice which shocked me, but I still didn't let my guard down because he was truly a Doctor Jekyll and Mister Hyde. He was buying me things without me asking for it, but my conscious was telling me don't take it, but I did and I definitely regretted it. Everything and anything he brought me he wanted it back every time we got into an argument or a fight. He would say give me back those shoes, pants or whatever he purchased, but I would say to him, "Take it. I don't care because any and everything you buy me, I can buy it myself because I have a job and I can afford it." When he would try to give me the stuff back days later, I would say, "No I don't want it because every time I turn around you always want it back. So just keep it."

He would say, "____ it. I'll throw it in the trash then." But I wouldn't say anything out loud. To myself I said, "I don't give a ____, your loss." One thing he hated was that I was independent and I didn't need to depend on him to take care of me. His life was all about selling drugs. He was a certified Brick Layer, but didn't put it to use. It just sat there in a folder collecting dust. One day I said to him, "Why don't you do something positive for once in your life and stop selling drugs?" He went off saying, "____ you ____. I'm my own man. Don't be

A Wasted 10 Years
Selena Walton

telling me what to do, you worry about yourself _____. You don't be saying that when you need some money."

I quickly said, "I won't ask you for another dime because you really hurt my feelings. When I owed you money, you call me up on my phone on my pay day saying 'I want my _____ _____ money today' like I'm some _____ on the street when I'm your wife."

Of course after I got that off my chest, he said, "So what. I don't give a ____. Do something about it if you don't like it." I just walked away and that was my mistake for turning my back on him because he punched me in back of the head and I lost my balance and fell to my knees. I got up off the floor and soon as I turned around he punched me in my eye causing me to be in a daze for a minute and the next thing I knew he punched me again in the same eye. I couldn't see nothing out of that eye. I looked in the mirror with my one good eye and one side of my face was nothing but blood. I was scared because I thought my eye was gone. I drove myself to the hospital and of course I still had my eye, but I had to get four stitches under my eye and three stitches over the top of my eye. This time I said, "Forget it. I'm going to my parent's house. I don't care if they see me like this." I was really tired of him doing this to me. I called my parents first to let them know what happened so I wouldn't take them by surprise. They immediately asked, "Did you call the police?"

A Wasted 10 Years
Selena Walton

I said, "No, I just want to come stay there for a while."

When I got there, they said, "Come on. You know you can come home any time." When I got there my parents were crushed and holding back tears. My son was staying with my parents at the time to finish out the school year. He saw my face when he got from school and asked me what happened. Of course I lied to him not wanting him to know the truth, but he looked at me with a look on his face that was saying I know you lying mom. I stuck with my story though. I went to lay down to get some rest and the next thing I know, flowers were being delivered to my parent's house. I told my dad, "I don't want it." He let the delivery person know to send it back. I stayed at my parent's house for a couple of days and I went right back to him after that. Of course I was out of work for a couple of weeks again. The whole time I was home, I was trying to come up with a story to tell my co-workers if any of my marks were still visible. When I got back to work, one of my co-workers asked, "Are you and your husband fighting?"

I said, "Why you ask me that?"

She said, "Because my husband fights me all the time, but I love it because it's a turn on." I just looked at her with a smile and said to myself, *"Maybe this is how it supposed to be in a marriage. She's an older lady and they said listen to your elders because they know best."* I never did answer her' cause deep down inside I thought

A Wasted 10 Years
Selena Walton

she was crazy or she couldn't get any other man. All day I was asking myself, "Will I become conditioned to a man fighting me and start thinking the same way she does? No I don't want a life like that."

Everything was peaches and cream for a while or should I say for about a couple of weeks until he came home one morning around four o'clock, an hour before I got up for work. He was making all kinds of noises in the house like he was trying to make me say something about it. He finally came in the bedroom and I could hear him moving around, then he sat on the edge of the bed not saying a word. All of a sudden he pulled the cover off me and I had my clothes on, of course I slept with clothes on because I didn't know what he would be up to once he got home. He immediately starting lashing out, calling me names and wanted to fight. I got up and started getting myself ready for work so I could hurry up and get out the house to avoid having to fight him. My heart was racing because I didn't know what he was going to do because he kept following me.

I said, "Please would you leave me alone?" I sat on the bed to put my socks on.

He pulled out his gun and put it to my head and said, "_____ I will kill you." Deep down inside I was a scared little girl asking, "Is this my last day and hour on earth? I won't be able to see my son graduate or see him having a family one day." The words that came out my mouth, wasn't what I was thinking inside. I said, "If you

A Wasted 10 Years
Selena Walton

going to kill me then kill me. Get it over with." He looked at me and then took the gun and hit me in my head. The only thing I felt was pain and tears. He continued to argue with me like nothing had just happened. I went back into the bathroom to wipe the tears from my eyes and when I turned the light on my white t-shirt was red from blood coming from my head. The blood that was coming down was taking over the tears I was shedding from the pain I was feeling. I went to feel my head and my hair sounded like a wet sponge because my hair was soaked with blood.

I screamed at him asking, "What in the hell have you done to my head?"

He said, "Let me see. Oh no, I think you need stitches."

I wasn't trying to go to the hospital again because that would have been my third time going because of abuse. I just put a towel around my head to soak up the blood and kept it on until I finished getting dressed for work, but I saw that my hair was still soaked with blood so I got another towel to put on my head. I left for work and when I got there I put my work hat on. I was at work for about twenty minutes and my head started to bleed more. I had to ask my supervisor could she come with me to the bathroom 'cause I needed to show her something. When I removed my hat and told her to look in my head, she was about to pass out. She said, "Oh my god, you have a big hole in your head. You

A Wasted 10 Years
Selena Walton

need stitches. What in the world happened? Never mind I already know that crazy fool did this to you. You need to leave him and call the police on him." Then she said, "You want me to drive you to the hospital?" I said, "No. I will take myself." So I left and went to the hospital and I ended up with six staples in my head from him hitting me in my head with his gun. When I walked out of the hospital he was outside in his car. "Come here." he said.

"What for?" I asked. He kept saying, "I'm so sorry. I don't know what got into me. I won't do it again. I'm just going to stop drinking because I know it's the alcohol that's causing me to act like that."

I said, "Stop blaming it on the liquor. You intended to hurt me, but that's okay. There's no use in you being with me when you don't trust me anyway."

"I do trust you. I say anything when I been drinking."

I said, "You right. The truth always comes out." I got in my car and went home. Yeah, I said home. I still stayed with him after that.

We eventually moved again, but this time back to the area where we were from, St. Mary's County, MD. Things still didn't change any. He would walk around without saying a word to me for days and days at a time. When I was asleep he would go through my phone looking at the contacts I had and would call the

A Wasted 10 Years
Selena Walton

men's numbers I had listed. I didn't know this until one day when I got to work, one of the guys asked, "Why you call me last night around 1 o'clock?"

I replied, "No I didn't. I was sleeping." The guy showed me on his phone, my number calling him. I just shook my head and said, "I know who did it."

When I got home I didn't say a word to him about it, but my phone rung and it was another guy. He said, "What's up Selena? I missed your call last night. Is everything good?"

I said, "Everything's cool." When I got off the phone I said something to him about going through my phone when I was asleep.

He said, "I didn't bother your phone."

"Whatever. Just leave my phone alone. I don't bother yours, don't bother mine." I walked off from him, but he just laughed. Then he made several statements wanting me to stoop to his level so we could fight, but I didn't give him that benefit. At this time my son was staying with us since I was back in my home town. So this particular night we got to arguing in the bedroom because I refused to have sex with him. That connection wasn't there anymore and I was at a point of no return. The argument lead out into the hallway and my son came out of nowhere and pulled a knife on him. My son said, "I'm tired of you messing with my mom. I know

A Wasted 10 Years
Selena Walton

you be fighting my mom. Why don't you leave? I hate you!"

He looked at my son like he wanted to hit him, but I got in front of my son and said, "If you touch my son, God as my witness. I will go to jail tonight because I will kill you! That's it, it's over! I don't want you anymore. I can't put up with you any longer." The next day I gave the landlord my 30 day notice. I was stunned that my son noticed, all this time that he was abusing me. That's what made me stick to my decision of leaving. You never know what your kids know. Even though we never fought in front of my son, he still knew that the harm being done to me was done by my ex-husband. I couldn't see my son suffer especially when I know how he feels. My ex didn't say a word to me once I gave the landlord the 30 day notice, but I didn't care because I was at a point of no return. When it was time to pay the rent, he said, "I hope you got money to pay your rent because I got my own place now, this your place not mine." I ignored him because I knew he was going to do that, I had that feeling, but again I was at a point of no return. I had the money which I know he was thinking I didn't have it, but I was two steps ahead of the game. When I got home he had already packed all his clothes and I was happy. I said, "When you leaving?"

He said, "_____ don't worry about me."

I said, "Trust and believe I'm not worried about you." He then left and went on about his business. I

A Wasted 10 Years
Selena Walton

didn't quite have peace of mind yet because I didn't know if he had an extra key made and was going to walk up in there when I was asleep and do something to me. All that ran thru my mind while I was still staying there. When my 30 days were up, I moved with my oldest sister because he didn't know where she lived. That's one thing about me, I never showed him where all my family and friends stayed just in case I needed to get away from him. Once I moved with my sister I had piece of mind and got myself plenty of rest. He kept calling my phone, but I didn't answer. I eventually turned my phone off and I got a good night's rest.

About two months later he went to jail, but not for abusing me. The first person he called was me and asked could I get his money and pay his lawyer. The first thing I said to him was, "Now you trust me and need me? The way you treated me I shouldn't do a damn thing for you, but I'm not you." I did it for him. I hated myself for doing it because I should of let him be on his own to find someone else to do it for him. Me stepping out of this toxic relationship was a big strain off my shoulders. I was in heaven thanking God for giving me the strength to put one foot in front of the other and leave this abusive man. Then it came down to me not being able to answer my own question, "Why am I still with him? I can do better." When I got to know the Lord, it was revealed to me that I wasn't put on this earth to be submissive to a man that's going to keep using me for a punching bag. Eventually I knew I had low self-esteem

A Wasted 10 Years
Selena Walton

once I got out of that 10 year abusive relationship. I met this guy and he wasn't any better than my ex because he was married and that was something I would never do. That is, have an affair with a married man. He wasn't an abusive man, but he wasn't mine. I was having an affair with this man for a little over two years. I would sit there and watch him lie to his wife on the phone saying he was working late, he loved her and at the same time he was telling me he was in love with me and wanted to leave his wife. I didn't fall for that. I started waking up, bringing my self-esteem back up and I met another guy that was single and trying to find the right woman to settle down with. He was so nice to me and knew how to treat a woman. I told the married man that it was over and I had met someone I truly liked and he was single. He was mad and looked at me with such rage in his eyes, but I stood my ground because I just knew he wanted to fight me. Instead he said, "How could you do that to me? I was leaving my wife for you. I love you and now you just going to step on my heart."

I said, "You have a wife to go home to. You have been having your cake and eating it too with the icing on it." I said, "If it wasn't for the low self-esteem, I wouldn't have been vulnerable from the start. I had fun with you, but this ride has come to an end."

I filed for a divorce and of course my ex-husband sent me a letter from prison calling me every name in the book except a child of God, but I didn't

A Wasted 10 Years
Selena Walton

care. I felt good about myself. To this day, the man I met was the man of my dreams and we got married. He loves me for who I am. I suffer with anxiety attacks really bad because of me going through the abuse for so many years, but he was right there for me, comforting me, not wanting to leave my side. He would tell me that I'm beautiful and I am somebody. Hearing that from him helped me out a lot. My husband helped me to a place of healing these old wounds that truly weren't healed because I never talked about my abuse openly, but now you can't stop me from talking about it. I thank God for sending this man to me.

Today I am a Motivational Speaker and Advocate of Domestic Violence. My mission is to inspire and motivate individuals through my story of surviving domestic violence and to encourage others to speak out because it could save a life.

A History of Battery
LJ Thomas

Visible, INvisibility

Am I invisible,
did no one hear my cries?
What once was love,
turned into pain, deceit, and lies.

What did I DO!!
to deserve your wrath?
This question I asked,
while picking myself up after the stormy aftermath.

I cleaned, I cooked,
took care of our five babies too
And my reward for being a good mother and wife to you
was black eyes, cracked ribs.
Please I beg of you, tell me what did I do?!!

WHY DID YOU HAVE SUCH DISREGUARD FOR ME?
That you would put your hands were they did not belong and would not set me free.
A prisoner I was for seventeen years,
through many heartbreaks and mountains of tears.

You damaged me,
my self-esteem
and you exchanged my love for you
and replaced it with fear.

Asoral Publishing

A History of Battery
LJ Thomas

I can still hear the WORDS you said to me
You're ugly, your nothing, who wants you but me?
So when I looked in the mirror
That's what I saw too,

But I was secretly making a plan,
and praying then leaving it in God's hands.
Now I stand tall here before you saying,
I made it out and with GOD'S HELP, so can you.

© Sandra Anderson

A History of Battery
LJ Thomas

Too Scared To Breathe

As I lay in this bed,

in this big empty room

I remember praying that you wouldn't come home.

To scared to move,

too scared to breathe

And I'm tortured still by my memories...

I remember your voice,

feel the pain and then

Reality snaps me back again...

Recalling the reason,

I lay here alone,

I'm relieved that you left

and glad that you're gone.

You caused me enough pain

to last my whole life

Though I have your last name...

I'm no longer your wife.

The divorce was far more

than a means to an end,

A History of Battery
LJ Thomas

It allowed me the chance

to start over again.

And now that I'm out,

I don't worry no more

About your outrage

when you walk through the door.

I'm safe and I'm happy.

I can do as I please…

But I'll never forget,

being too scared to breathe…

Dedicated to all the women who suffer abuse at the hands that vowed to love them…

© Sandra Krajewski 11/27/11

Asoral Publishing

A History of Battery
LJ Thomas

A History of Battery

By LJ Thomas

Asoral Publishing
36

A History of Battery
by LJ Thomas

Not everyone in an abusive relationship experiences physical violence. Until I started doing this book, I believed I had never been in a domestically abusive relationship. The co-authors and my research have opened my eyes. Here are the things I have seen related to this subject.

Grandma & Granddaddy

I remember every Friday my grandmother would come home from work and cook fish, rice and cornbread. I would stand in the doorway and watch her cook dinner. I can't count the number of times that my grandfather came home from work starting trouble. Every week he would come in smelling like liquor. He stuttered when he spoke, so it was worse on Friday evenings. On one particular occasion, grandma was in the kitchen cooking, as usual. She was tired. You could see it in her body language, but she was making dinner anyway. Granddaddy came in from work bugging her. I could tell when he was home because I could smell the liquor on him, even from the kitchen located at the back of the small house.

A History of Battery
LJ Thomas

I couldn't have been more than 4 years old. We spent a lot of time at my grandma's house. And I was always right up under her, at least as much as I could be. She was the only grandmother on my mother's side. That made her even more special to me.

I distinctly remember my grandmother saying, "Leave me alone."

My grandfather was determined to get on her nerves. He walked over to her and tried to stop her from cooking. Since he had just come home from work, you would think he would be ready to eat and let her finish cooking.

"Leave me alone Buddy. Go to bed." She said without turning around. She was frying the fish and I remember thinking that the grease might burn her if he didn't leave her alone. He was pulling on her and doing everything he could to get her to stop cooking. My grandmother was not a little woman. She wasn't talk, but she was strong. She was a hard worker and this was in the 70's in the south, so she was used to using her strength. A person looking at her could easily be deceived about her strength

A History of Battery
LJ Thomas

Granddaddy said something else and I remember him touching grandma again, but I'm not sure what was going on. Then grandma said, "I'm tired. Go on to bed and leave me alone."

I don't remember the exact conversation, at least until things moved into the living room located at the front of the house. My grandma was cursing my granddaddy out and he was doing the same to her. Then, all of a sudden, the two of them were locked in a frenzied embrace. Granddaddy was trying to choke grandma as he had his hands around her throat. Grandma was trying to push him off of her. Even though he wasn't a big man, he had some strength, too. The next thing I knew the two of them were on the floor and they had fallen over the coffee table. My grandma was on the bottom. I was scared. What would I do without my grandma? I mean, this happened every Friday, but it always ended with granddaddy going to bed after grandma cursed him out and threatened him. Once he went to bed, she would go about her other duties in the house and finally sit down and relax. He had not done anything like this that I had never seen this before. I saw that my grandma was in trouble and that jolted me into action. I didn't know what to do. I was yelling for him to leave her alone. I told him to get off my grandma. Finally, I picked up a vase that had

A History of Battery
LJ Thomas

fallen to the floor and hit my granddaddy in the head as hard as I could I jumped back after I hit him because I thought he might try to choke me and I knew I couldn't fight him off. I was hoping he would let my grandma go. It worked!

"Wha wha wha whatcha do that for?" he screamed through his stutter holding his head. My grandma pushed him off of her and got to her feet. First she told me to get out of the room. Then I heard her order my granddaddy to go to bed. I guess he did. A while later I remember seeing him in the bed sleeping. I didn't feel bad about hitting him, but I was glad I helped my grandmother. I was tired of him coming home from work every Friday drunk and starting a fight. You would think he'd learn that he couldn't beat my grandma when he was drunk, but he never did.

Grandma let me come back in the living room and I noticed that she had straightened all the furniture. I didn't see the vase or the pieces that had tumbled to the floor when I hit granddaddy. She and I never spoke about the incident. To this day we have never talked about it. I finally told my mother once I was grown, but I just mentioned that I hot granddaddy when he was fighting grandma when I

A History of Battery
LJ Thomas

was little. She asked for details, but I would not give them to her.

One day when I was around five years old, granddaddy said he was going to the store and never came back. I was glad because it meant that my grandma didn't have to fight every Friday or at all for that matter. As a small child, I thought he might have left because I hit him, but as I grew up, I realized that was not the case.

A History of Battery
LJ Thomas

Mom and Dad

I don't know how old I was when I saw my parent's fighting, but I was younger than five. I know this because my daddy left when I was five years old. I remember where we lived, that it was late at night, that my siblings were all asleep and watching them as they fought from one room to another. I remember getting out of bed to go to the bathroom. As I walked out of the bedroom, I glanced into the living room because the light was on. I was surprised to see my 5'5" mother jump up and slap my 6'3" father in the face. She slapped him so hard that his head turned. I was so shocked that I just stood in place and watched. Something must be really wrong for my mother to fight. My father retaliated and the fight was on! They rolled around from room to room fighting. I remember my mother looking up at me in wonder. "What are you doing up?" she asked.

"I had to pee." I replied.

"Well go back to bed." she ordered as they fought. I did not want to because I wanted to make sure both my parents were okay, but I obeyed and that was that. I didn't know what happened for that to take place. But, later in life, I learned the back

A History of Battery
LJ Thomas

story and found out that my father had actually hit my mother first and she was defending herself. I'm proud of her for that. She always taught me to defend myself and never let a man think that he can fight me or abuse me without consequences.

Years later we moved from South Carolina to Maryland and I witnessed another altercation between my parents. They had reconciled after years of being separated. We moved to where my dad was so he wouldn't have to find a find a new job. I did not want to move. At twelve years old, I was growing up and understand more about life and relationships. I thought it was a mistake and I let my mother know how I felt.

I remember my father coming in from work one day. I was excited because even though we lived into a small 2 bedroom apartment, I rarely got to see him. He left for work very early as a construction worker and when he came home in the evening, he went to their bedroom and stayed there (I used to think that having a house full of children was too much for him. We are not loud, but we were active kids and since we were in a new city, we were getting used to things, just like him. We did not know how to act with a man in the house). Anyway, my mom had not found a job yet, so she

A History of Battery
LJ Thomas

was in the kitchen making dinner, rather than me (in South Carolina, I had done the cooking since I was eight years old and my mom had to work). Earlier in the week I had heard my mother tell my father that he needed to find a larger place for all of us. I didn't hear the rest of it, but I know she was very unhappy with all of us crowded in a small 2 bedroom apartment. (It was supposed to be temporary).

My father seemed to be in a bad mood as he walked into the kitchen where my mom was making dinner on this particular day. He had come into the apartment with a frown on his face. So I made up my mind to be as quiet as I could. I was standing in the doorway because I've always been a daddy's girl, so I was always tagging along with him when I could. My parents were speaking in hushed tones, so I couldn't hear what was being said. That is, until my mother reached over and put her left hand on the butcher knife on the counter next to her and said, "Leave me alone, Tim." She never even looked up from what she was doing. I had no idea what was happening, but I could tell it was serious.

My father got a look of surprise on his face, mumbled something and walked out of the kitchen. He didn't even notice me standing there. Maybe he remembered the fight they had when I was a little girl and did not want a repeat. He went to the bedroom and a few minutes later he came out and left the apartment. Meanwhile, my mother finished making dinner and called us to come eat. She didn't seem upset or angry. But, looking at her face, she had a lot on her mind. As a twelve year old, I had no idea about married life and how things were handled, even though I thought I understood relationships. After all, my parents had been separated most of my life. Judging by my father's behavior, they wouldn't be together much longer, either.

A History of Battery
LJ Thomas

Dot & James

I must have been about five or six years old. My mother had a family member who used to come visit us. I can't remember if she was a cousin or what, but I liked her. She was not much bigger than me and she was a grown lady. She always walked to our house and this didn't seem strange, since we always walked where we had to go. Sometimes she would come with her husband and sometimes she would be alone. Her husband was a big tall man.

I always knew when they were coming, because I would hear them before I ever saw them. He would be yelling at her, cussing her out and calling her names. I remember one time, they were walking along and she was carrying an arm full of stuff, but he wasn't carrying anything. He was yelling at her to hurry up. But anybody could see that she was tired carrying all that heavy stuff by herself. He didn't care. Instead, he yelled, cursed and screamed at her as they walked down the street. He even pushed her which caused her to stumble. Then said, "You better not fall. If you do, you gonna pick up all that stuff off the ground and nothing better be broke!"

A History of Battery
LJ Thomas

She whimpered, but steadied herself so she wouldn't drop anything.

"Come on slow poke!" he shouted as they came closer to our house.

There must have been times when she would come to visit during the day without him, but I don't remember that. I do remember her coming to our house late one night and she was staggering. Even at this age, I knew that meant she was drunk. But then, I thought she might be drinking to forget the pain and the times that he hit her. She was so small, barely five foot tall and a petite woman. She would take the beatings because I remember her coming to the house with black eyes and bloody noses. This was during the 70's so the laws were completely different. I remember being in bed one night and I heard my mother talking. I was always curious, so I got up to see who it was. It was Dot sitting in a chair and my mother was talking to her as she cleaned up her face. I was so worried about her. Her eye was swollen and she was bleeding.

"What are you doing up? My mother asked.

"I have to go to the bathroom." I replied as I starred at Dot's bloody face.

"Then go and go back to bed." my mother ordered.

I did as I was told, but once I got back in the bed, I couldn't go to sleep. I kept seeing Dot's face. I must have drifted off to sleep, because when I woke up Dot was gone. My mother didn't mention what I saw and neither did I. But, that image has stayed with me throughout my life. Unfortunately, Dot was killed at a club. I remember thinking that at least she didn't have to suffer through James beating on her anymore.

Fran & Dave

As a preteen, we lived on a small street in a fairly quiet community. The houses were close enough that you could hear loud noises and voices next door. On one side of us was a family with a few girls and one boy. They stayed to themselves, but one of the daughters and I played together often. On the other side of us lived a small family, husband, wife and two small children. My mother was close with the wife, so she would come over and visit sometimes.

A History of Battery
LJ Thomas

The way our house was made, my small bedroom was on the side closest to their house. So, I heard the really loud noises. Sometimes I would be in my room trying to sleep and I'd hear, "Stop Dave!" "No!".

Other times I could hear something being thrown against something and I would hear screams. One night I heard a combination of the two and about an hour later, as I was looking out of the window, I saw a figure run across the yard.

I peeked down the hall and watched my mother open our back door. The lady who lived next door was covered in blood and crying. She was a small lady but her husband was a big man. At the age of nine or ten, I didn't fully understand what had happened. But, I knew that she was running from her husband and he had hurt her really bad this time.

I have known this woman my entire life and I am amazed that she survived the beatings. She and Dave divorced and I was so happy when I found out. I always wished there was something I could do to help her. When my mother would clean her up, I tried to stay quiet and in the background. Most of the time, my mother never knew I was awake and

A History of Battery
LJ Thomas

saw what happened. The sights and sounds of beatings and images of her being battered have always stayed with me.

A History of Battery
LJ Thomas

Ron & I

As a teenager, I was concerned with making the right choices. However, I met a boy as a child, to whom I was, I thought jokingly, promised to marry. Our parents went to high school together and just before we moved from South Carolina to Maryland, the two of them decided we should get married later in life. I guess they thought that because the two of them were such good friends, that their children would make a good couple. Humph.

Naturally, I didn't think much of it. We moved north and returned to the south 3 years later (thank goodness). He was nowhere to be found since they had moved away as well. However, the following school year, they returned to the area. We live in the same school district and attended the same high school. I was a quiet girl in school, but everyone knew him. He loved attention. Imagine my surprise when he came up to me at school and asked me to be his girlfriend. I gave him a 'you must be crazy look'. He stated his case as to why and mentioned that technically we were already engaged. I ignored him and went about my business. He had grown into a tall young man, while I was a small young lady and barely 100

A History of Battery
LJ Thomas

pounds. I was always a quiet person, so I wasn't accustomed to someone constantly asking me to be in a relationship. No one at school paid me any attention and I liked it that way. The fact that I only had a few close friends suited me just fine.

However seeing Ron at school and religious meetings a few times a week, his request got to be a problem. He never missed an opportunity remind me of the agreement between our parents. Finally, one day at school, I was on my way to class and saw him from a distance. I calmly walked over to him said, "Yes." and walked off. Ron was very popular at school and this turned me off. I did not like attention.

He called me later that evening. I didn't dislike him, he was okay as a person, but I hated the assumption that we were supposed to be in a serious relationship based on what our parents felt and what happened years ago. I don't like for people to tell me what to do and not take my thoughts are feelings into consideration.

Anyway, the conversation went okay and the next day he came to my class and walked with me. The kind of thing a "real" boyfriend does. I was shocked. I figured he just did it for show and that he

A History of Battery
LJ Thomas

would soon stop after he accomplished whatever his goal was. This was the beginning of my junior year in high school. The relationship went on, off and on, until after we graduated.

I remember an incident when I had early dismissal from school because I had accumulated a large number of credits and my last class was study hall. I would go home, put my books down, then walk to the elementary school and pick up my little sister. On this particular day, I went inside, dropped my books, then changed into a pair of shorts because it was hot. I walked to the mailbox at the street to get the mail. I followed my daily routine and Ron called later that afternoon when he got home from school. This was in the 80's and before cellphones. The latest thing was pagers.

"I thought I told you not to wear those shorts outside." Ron said after I said hello. He didn't have a laugh or joking tone and I knew he was dead serious.

"What are you talking about?" I asked baffled at his question.

"You went to the mailbox today in those blue shorts that I told you not to wear!" He yelled.

A History of Battery
LJ Thomas

At this point, I realized he was watching me. I immediately got angry. "How do you know what I had on? Weren't you at school?" I asked. I was upset that he thought he could order me to do or not do things simply because we are in a 'relationship'.

"Yeah, I was. Don't worry about how I know. I know everything you do. You don't have any secrets from me. Remember that." He said in a threatening tone. For a quick second, I got a little scared. But then I realized that he and I are the same age and I don't have to take that from him. So we argued. We did this a lot. As a compromise, I agreed not to wear the shorts outside the house and he agreed to stop spying on me. Although I knew it was a lie and he was still going to continue, but just wouldn't let me find out. The school year ended and during the summer, he would stop by for a few minutes when he was either on break or on his way to work.

One day he stopped by and of course all of my siblings were at home as well. My mother did not allow any boys to come by the house to visit. They used to call it 'taking company'. Since all of my siblings knew Ron, there was no problem with him coming in and visiting for a short time. He teased my brothers for a little while and then asked

A History of Battery
LJ Thomas

me to walk with him to the bedroom I shared with my sisters. I did with no problem. But once we were in the room and he asked me to come to him as he sat on a chair, I was hesitant. I don't know, but something was different and I could feel it in the air.

"Are you afraid of me? You act like you're scared to come here." He casually asked as he looked at me. I don't know why I didn't want to go to him. We had argued the day before on the phone, but that was normal. He was always affectionate the next day when I saw him at school, but we weren't in school right now. Something was different, but I couldn't put my finger on what it was. This visit was a surprise.

"No. I'm not afraid of you." I quietly answered.

"Then come here. Don't you want to hug your future husband? I just want you to sit on my lap before I go to work." He said in a sincere tone. This didn't seem so unreasonable. Besides, we were not sexually active and he wasn't asking for much. Slowly I walked over to him thinking that I was being silly. True to his word, I sat on his lap for a few minutes and gave him a hug. Suddenly, he

A History of Battery
LJ Thomas

stood up holding me in his arms like a small child. He carried me to my bed and tossed me on it. Then he yelled for my brother to bring him a belt. My brother had no idea what was going on. He didn't bring a belt. He brought a plastic baseball bat instead at Ron's request.

I was trying to figure out why he wanted the belt and now the bat for, but I soon found out. He swiftly flipped me onto my stomach and held me there with his hand on the back of my neck. The next thing I knew, he was hitting me with the bat on my butt. At first I thought he was just playing around, that is, until it really started to hurt. I was screaming for him to stop and when my siblings came to see what the problem was, he convinced them that we were playing, so they left without doing anything to help me. Once he had given what he considered a good beating to me, he stopped, dropped the bat and walked out. I was left on the bed in pain and crying. As I lay there, I realized that he gave me a beating as a parent disciplines a child. He gave me no explanation as to why he did that, although that would not have made it any better.

I got so angry, that I got up off the bed and walked to our room door to see if he had left. I saw him walking down the hall. I was angry, so I ran as

A History of Battery
LJ Thomas

fast as I could and hit him in the back with all the strength I had. He fell forward and stumbled down the steps onto the ground with the wind knocked out of him for a minute. When he got up, he got in his car and went to work. He didn't say anything to me as he walked to the car or anything. He just left. We never spoke about the incident and he probably doesn't remember it. When I took my shower that night before bed, I was very sore, but I noticed the bruises on my butt. I never told my mother about what happened. I was sore for a few days and it took a while for the bruising to go away, every time I sat down, I got a vision of the lesson he wanted me to learn. We are not in contact, so to this day, I have no idea what the lesson was or if I learned it.

Later that summer before my senior year of high school, I met someone who became a friend. He and I would talk on the phone sometimes, but that was it. We weren't in a relationship. How could I be? Each time Ron and I broke up, for some reason no one else ever showed any interest in me, well no one at school. I didn't think much about it at the time, but now I wonder. He was popular at school with everyone.

So, one day after the school year had begun, I was talking to this guy in the hallway between

A History of Battery
LJ Thomas

classes. Our classes were near each other and we were just making small talk before the late bell rang. Out of nowhere, Ron walked up to me, lifted me from the floor (holding me under my arms), carried me into my classroom, put me in my seat and said, "Don't you move until the bell rings."

"You're not my daddy. Don't tell me what to do!" I screamed as he started to leave the room.

"You heard what I said." he uttered in a quiet voice without missing a beat and walked out of the room.

I was so angry at him for embarrassing me and trying to tell me what to do. Obviously he didn't realize that I wasn't his child. It didn't help that some of the girls in class made comments like "Aww that is so cute" "He really loves you" and other things. The whole time, I was thinking, he has lost his mind and he must not know who I am. I decided that when I talked to him, we were gonna have a serious conversation about what he did.

Like clockwork he called me once he got home from school. Oh, we had a conversation all right. We argued and I hung up. I let him know that I was not a child and he was going to treat me with respect or that would be the end. Surprisingly, by

A History of Battery
LJ Thomas

this time, I had actually developed romantic feelings for him. Go figure.

I didn't expect to see him when the bell rang for us to go to our first class the next day, but there he was waiting outside the door. We walked along in quietness, neither of us mentioning what happened the day before. It bothered me that he was obviously angry with me. So, when we entered the stairway, I stopped him so we could kiss and makeup. I guess it worked because he was fine after that. He was back to teasing and picking on everyone.

Later that same school year I was assaulted by the guy that he didn't want me to talk to. Ron found out about it and came to talk with me. I just knew he was gonna fuss and blame me, but instead, he was angry with the guy and looking for chances to beat him up. I begged him not to and to let the police handle it. Finally he agreed and that was the end of that.

After we graduated from high school, he and I kept seeing each other. Then one day he introduced me to a young lady that he said, "My mother wants me to date her." I was nice about it and since he and I worked very close to each other,

A History of Battery
LJ Thomas

I would see him all the time. He would walk past my store and look to see what I was doing, but not come inside. On this day, he came inside. I was angry because I saw him at our religious meeting with her again and he didn't look like he was being forced to do anything. I had already made up my mind about what I was going to do and the opportunity presented itself.

He walked up with his confident stride and my co-worker asked if he was my boyfriend, I replied in the affirmative, and said, "But not for long." She went to her desk as I walked over to the counter. He acted like there was nothing wrong with his new girlfriend sitting with him and his family behind me at the meeting. So, I mentioned it and he gave me some song and dance about what his mother wanted to happen. When he finished I calmly looked him in the eye and said, "I hope the two of you have a wonderful life and beautiful children. Tell her that if there is anything she wants to know about you that she can give me a call." Then I walked off and left him standing at the counter with a dumbfounded look on his face.

I wasn't concerned about the fact that there were several co-workers standing close enough to hear what happened. I didn't care about his feelings.

A History of Battery
LJ Thomas

I was fed up with his lies, cheating, controlling ways and everything else. After I had done this, I felt so much better. It was like a weight had been lifted. Here I was at nineteen years old in a relationship that was wrong on more than one level. I had been ignoring the signs and realized that I needed to get out while I could. I finally realized that if I married him, that my life would be miserable and I did not want that. Though I do not believe he would have beat me the way I had seen some when beaten as I grew up, I definitely felt it would be an abusive relationship. I was not going to have that.

Liz & Joe

My Aunt Liz was a tall woman with a heart of gold when it came to us. She would help buy school clothes, and more for us when my parents were separated. She would have us over for dinner every Sunday. It was during this time that I really saw how she treated Uncle Joe. I could never figure out why Aunt Liz had a California king sized bed in her bedroom and Uncle Joe had a walk-in closet side bedroom next to hers. He had a twin sized bed and a little TV and a chair in his room. He spent all of his time in there. He even ate his meals in there on a TV table. This just didn't make any sense to me, but I never said anything.

We used to spend a lot of time at Aunt Liz and Uncle Joe's house when we lived in Maryland. So we saw and heard a lot. I used to hear Aunt Liz cussing Uncle Joe out, calling him names, then ordering him to go to the store and buy things. Uncle Joe would go to the store and get what she wanted. I could not understand this. I would not have done it after the way she talked to him.

We moved back to South Carolina and after a few years, so did Aunt Liz and Uncle Joe. I was so happy that I would get to see them on a regular basis again. By this time, I was in high school. So my mom usually took us to see them every month or so. Their place was small so we didn't spend the night. But, Aunt Liz always wanted to make dinner. Again, I noticed that they had separate bedrooms and she was still yelling at him and he was still buying her whatever she wanted. This was baffling to me. But, I know he really loved her and she really loved him. She would get up and cook even when she was in extreme pain. Their place was small, but she was always make sure it was clean

A History of Battery
LJ Thomas

(as much as she could) and always cooked what he wanted.

It wasn't until the family was sitting around talking one day after Uncle Joe had died, that I found out that Aunt Liz used to physically hit Uncle Joe. I even heard the story of how she broke both his wrists and they were in casts when I was a baby. There was a comparison of me and Uncle Joe and how we held our hands. I don't know why she broke his wrists, but that's what happened.

A History of Battery
LJ Thomas

Maggie & JB

My grandmother had a sister named Maggie. She was amazing. I used to love to visit her because he had a tree in her front yard that was perfect for climbing. Every chance I got, I was in that tree.

One day we arrived and we were going to spend the weekend with Aunt Maggie. I was excited about this because not only would I get to climb the tree, but she was an amazing cook. She made the best homemade cakes and I was looking forward to this.

We must have gotten there on a Friday evening. I don't remember where my mom was going, but I remember that there were only five of us, which means that my baby sister was younger than seven years old. Normally we all slept in the living room on the floor. It was a big room or at least to a child of nine or ten, it was huge.

So, Aunt Maggie was in the kitchen making breakfast when we woke up. I think it was the smell of the food that woke us up. We all got up, washed up and changed our clothes before he sat down to eat. I remember uncle JB sitting at the table. He was

A History of Battery
LJ Thomas

a quiet man. He never said much. But Aunt Maggie was a talker. After we finished our food, Aunt Maggie told us to go outside and play. Yay! I went directly to the tree and started climbing. After I was about half way up, I heard loud voices coming from the house. My siblings heard it as well, but I made sure they did not go back in the house.

After we had been outside for a while, Aunt Maggie came to the front door and told us we can come inside for a snack. Uncle JB was still sitting at the kitchen table. When we came into the house and Aunt Maggie walked in the kitchen behind us, she yelled at Uncle JB and sold him to get his stupid self up, so we can sit down and eat. Uncle JB did not say anything back to Aunt Maggie, but he shot her a look that said, 'You are on thin ice'. Aunt Maggie saw it but didn't say anything. The rest of the day, we stayed outside playing until time for dinner. We heard loud voices. It finally got quiet between them when we went to bed. The next day, which was Sunday, Aunt Maggie got up, made breakfast and got ready for church. She left and we stayed at the house with Uncle JB. He talked to us and played with us. I kind of felt sorry for him because Aunt Maggie was always calling him

A History of Battery
LJ Thomas

names and I know how I felt when someone called me names.

I learned later in life that the two of them used to fight all the time and Aunt Maggie was the one who was always physical. That bothered because Uncle JB was such a nice man and he worked hard at the railroad. I did not think Aunt Maggie treated him fairly. But he loved her and stayed with her until he died.

A History of Battery
LJ Thomas

My Marriage

First let me say that I am married to a wonderful man. He is kind, considerate and loving to me. He is a protector and respectful to women. However, I have mistreated him in the past. Writing this book helped me to understand something about myself. ***I was an abuser*** and I am ashamed of it. But, if admitting this to myself and others helps even one person, then it is worth it.

I knew of family members (women) who were abusive and I witnessed some of it. But, I never thought of myself in this light. I was wrong. I was not verbally, emotionally, financially or psychologically abusive. However, I did lash out physically a few times. This was wrong and unacceptable behavior. There is never a time to put your hands on someone else in violence unless you are defending yourself and the moves are defensive.

As in any marriage, there are ups and downs, good and bad times. A few times during our downs, I have become so angry that I have physically hit my husband. I am not proud of this. I should have never allowed myself to lose control to the point that I hit my husband. Did I have a right to be angry? Yes. Was violence the answer? No. Did I

A History of Battery
LJ Thomas

feel better after I hit him? No. On one occasion, I hit him repeatedly, then threw my clothes in some trash bags, jumped in my car and left. When I thought about where I was and what I was doing, I was in the next state. I had left my children home with him knowing he had to go to work. But anger had made me make irrational and poor decisions.

I corrected my thought process and went home. Was I still angry? Definitely. But, I had to get control of the anger and my emotions. It was difficult, but I did it. Eventually my husband and I talked the next day and started working on the problem.

Another time, my husband got angry with me and put his finger in my face. Before I knew it I had pushed his hand out of the way and in reflex he grabbed me around the throat. That was all I needed to start punching with everything I had. I realized I was out of control when I went into the kitchen and got a butcher knife. It was hearing my children move around upstairs that made me stop and think. I put the knife back and went upstairs to talk to my children. Later that day, my husband and I had a talk and we expressed where both of us were coming from. We made up and that has never been an issue again. My husband is a gentleman. He has

A History of Battery
LJ Thomas

never put his hands on me in a way that I do not like. Even when I have hit him, he has never hit me back. Based on the things I have seen growing up and the values it had instilled in me, this is amazing. He is amazing.

I examined my behavior as I wrote this book and realized that I became physical while angry. True, the anger may have been warranted, but the violence was not. It never has been and never should have been used. Violence does not equal love. Sometimes a person can be an abuser and not realize it. But, that doesn't make it right. My aunts were dead wrong for the way they treated their husbands. Physical, verbal and psychological abuse is not the answer and it is never good. But, I learned from them. I saw what not to do to my husband. But I was still caught off guard when I became angry. To help fix the problem, I have gone to anger management, and I stop and think before I take any action. I think of how I would feel if my husband was hitting on me. This has helped tremendously.

I love my husband and I am in love with him. I would not be able to live with myself if I hurt him to the point that he died because I could not control my anger. The bottom line is that even if you are an abuser, you can get help and you can change. ***They key is wanting to and doing it.*** Admit that you have a problem and take the necessary steps to correct it. You can do it!

Remember, love is not abusive. Instead it conquers all.

Poetry Wisdom and Encouragement
By Herman H.

Don't

I don't let shit surprise me!
Think I've seen and done it all.

I can see the bigger picture, so
I just overlook the small.

The Devil don't take breaks, he
Stay open 24/7, I've been to hell
And back, Now I'm tryna get to
Heaven

He'll use your family, money, he
Will even use your friends, just
Tell them you ain't bout that
Life and watch how fast they
Change.

Don't let anything define you and
Don't do nothing you'll regret

Because they want to see you fail
And they would love to see you
Sweat

Don't let them shake you, and
Don't let no one change your
Mind

Poetry Wisdom and Encouragement
By Herman H.

If you believe that you can do
It. I believe you will be fine.

© Herman H.

So Far from Perfect

I'm so far from perfect, but I
Made it thru the storm, I was
Weak and I was lost but I'm
Back and standing strong

I was standing on the edge,
matter of fact, I lost all hope
but I put my faith in God and my
spirit wasn't broke

I was so hurt and so alone and
I never understood why, when
Everybody fell off, God was
Still right by my side.

I was ashamed and I was afraid
And I just wanted it to end
I could not forgive myself, so
How could God forgive my sin

I was in a bad situation, nor
The reason for my pain, I only

Poetry Wisdom and Encouragement
By Herman H.

Wanted to be happy, I just wanted
Shit to change!!

Believe me you, I'm far from perfect
But I do the best I can, I work
To be a better person and strive
To be a better man

© Herman H.

Poetry Wisdom and Encouragement
By Herman H.

Be Thankful

You best be thankful your still
Breathing, everyday somebodies
Grieving

So much hatred, so much pain,
Good people dying for no reason

You hate your mother and your
Mad, because you never knew
Your dad

I know you don't want to hear
Me preach, I learned the hard
Way in the streets

Because I had to fee my children
even if I didn't eat

And believe me I'm not perfect, but
If you ask me it was worth it

I've been there and I've done that
And you just now scratching the
Surface

don't you think it's time for
change, you so mysterious and
strange

Asoral Publishing

Poetry Wisdom and Encouragement
By Herman H.

Not a drop of motivation, no desire
To succeed, satisfied with what
You have, no idea of what you need.

So confused, so brainwashed and
Nothing to aspire to, there just
Doing what they learned as a child
From watching you

Fake friends, no goals, low self
Esteem, they just fall back and get
A check instead of getting up and
Chasing dreams

Ask this question, will yourself
Your situation ever change, if you
Want to make it work, then you
Then you have to change the game

Don't sit around, nor wait
Around and you don't have time
To play

Tomorrow isn't promised, so
Please get it done today

© Herman H.

Poetry Wisdom and Encouragement
By Herman H.

Move Mountains

I was born to move mountains
And you're content and standing
Still

So quick to be fake, to fake to
Be real

I will not let you destroy any
Thing I work to build

I've been at my lowest low and
It's a blessing that I survived.

Celebrating 50 years and I thank
God that I'm still alive

I just stay focused on my mission
And I strive to reach mu goals

I refuse to let you stop me and
I will never sell my soul

Because I can move mountains
And I will not let you destroy

My will, my faith, my determination
And you will never steal my joy

Asoral Publishing

Poetry Wisdom and Encouragement
By Herman H.

© Herman H.

𝒜soral 𝒫ublishing
77

Poetry Wisdom and Encouragement
By Herman H.

Why Not

Why not just do things different,
Why won't you just try some thing
New

How you choose to write your story
Is entirely up to you

With so many opportunities and
With so much room for change

Yu really can't afford to gamble
And your life is not a game

The things we want in life always
Come before our needs

If you believe you have the power
There's no way you can't succeed

Don't ever be just satisfied
Strive for bigger and better goals

Work your plan, then plan our
Work and just let the truth be
Told

It's not as hard as you think,
You just have to figure it out

Poetry Wisdom and Encouragement
By Herman H.

Then just refrain from doing
Anything that's not good for
Your health

I'll keep praying for you bro.,
Because I believe that you can
Make it

Sometimes we only get one
Shot, so don't be afraid to take
It

© Herman H.

Asoral Publishing

Types of Domestic Violence

All kinds of abuse are difficult to experience. Listed below are definitions of types of abuse for easy identification. Each type of abuse is serious and no one deserves to experience it.

Emotional Abuse/Verbal Abuse

These are non-physical behaviors such as threats, insults, constant monitoring or "checking in," excessive texting, humiliation, intimidation or isolation.

Stalking

When a person is being repeatedly watched, followed or harassed.

Financial Abuse

The practice of using money or access to accounts to exert power and control over a partner.

Physical Abuse

This is any intentional use of physical force with the intent to cause fear or injury, like hitting, shoving, biting, strangling, kicking or using a weapon.

Types of Domestic Violence

Sexual Abuse

Includes any action that impacts a person's ability to control their sexual activity or the circumstances in which sexual activity occurs, including restricting access to birth control or condoms. This includes ignoring someone's refusal to engage in sexual activities by repeatedly using emotional, verbal or physical pressure.

Digital Abuse

The use of technology such as texting and social networking to bully, harass, stalk or intimidate a partner. This behavior is frequently a form of verbal or emotional abuse perpetrated through technology.

Source: Helpguide.org

Types of Domestic Violence

Signs of an Abusive Relationship

When a person is in an abusive relationship, they often do not realize it. However, the most recognizable sign is fear of your partner.

If you feel like you have to 'walk on egg shells' around your partner and constantly watch what you say and do or he/she will blow up, then there is a good chance that the relationship is unhealthy and abusive. Other signs include a partner who belittles you, is controlling and someone who tries to invoke feelings of self-loathing, helplessness or desperation in you.

SIGNS THAT YOU'RE IN AN ABUSIVE RELATIONSHIP	
Your Inner Thoughts and Feelings	**Your Partner's Belittling Behavior**
Do you: feel afraid of your partner much of the time?	**Does your partner:** humiliate or yell at you?
avoid certain topics out of fear of angering your partner?	criticize you and put you down?

Types of Domestic Violence

feel that you can't do anything right for your partner?	treat you so badly that you're embarrassed for your friends or family to see?
believe that you deserve to be hurt or mistreated?	ignore or put down your opinions or accomplishments?
wonder if you're the one who is crazy?	blame you for their own abusive behavior?
feel emotionally numb or helpless?	see you as property or a sex object, rather than as a person?
Your Partner's Violent Behavior or Threats	**Your Partner's Controlling Behavior**
Does your partner:	**Does your partner:**
have a bad and unpredictable temper?	act excessively jealous and possessive?
hurt you, or threaten to hurt or kill you?	control where you go or what you do?
threaten to take your children away or harm them?	keep you from seeing your friends or family?
threaten to commit suicide if you leave?	limit your access to money, the phone, or the car?
force you to have sex?	limit your access to money, the phone, or

Types of Domestic Violence

	the car?
destroy your belongings?	constantly check up on you?

Types of Domestic Violence

Warning Signs

Asoral Publishing

Recognizing the warning signs of domestic violence and abuse

It's impossible to know with certainty what goes on behind closed doors, but there are some telltale signs and symptoms of emotional abuse and domestic violence. If you witness any warning signs of abuse in a friend, family member, or co-worker, take them very seriously.

General warning signs of domestic abuse

People who are being abused may:

- Seem afraid or anxious to please their partner

- Go along with everything their partner says and does

- Check in often with their partner to report where they are and what they're doing

- Receive frequent, harassing phone calls from their partner

- Talk about their partner's temper, jealousy, or possessiveness

Types of Domestic Violence

Warning signs of physical violence

People who are being physically abused may:

- Have frequent injuries, with the excuse of "accidents"

- Frequently miss work, school, or social occasions, without explanation

- Dress in clothing designed to hide bruises or scars (e.g. wearing long sleeves in the summer or sunglasses indoors)

Warning signs of isolation

People who are being isolated by their abuser may:

- Be restricted from seeing family and friends

- Rarely go out in public without their partner

- Have limited access to money, credit cards, or the car

The psychological warning signs of abuse

People who are being abused may:

- Have very low self-esteem, even if they used to be confident

- Show major personality changes (e.g. an outgoing person becomes withdrawn)

- Be depressed, anxious, or suicidal

Verbal & Emotional Abuse

Verbal and emotional abuse in a marriage is such a covert form of domestic violence and abuse, that many people aren't able to recognize they are a victim. A spouse may have a feeling that something is wrong. They may feel stressed out; a sense of depression; anxiety but they can't quite identify what is causing those feelings.

Are You a Victim of Emotional Abuse?

Emotional abuse is crippling. It robs a person of their self-esteem, the ability to think rationally, confidence in themselves and their independence and autonomy.

How Can Someone Identify and Respond to Verbal Abuse?

Types of Domestic Violence

Verbal abuse is the use of words to punish and control a spouse or partner. Screaming, yelling, cursing are all signs of a verbally abusive relationship.

Is Screaming and Yelling Verbal Abuse?

Example "My wife is constantly screaming and yelling. The least little thing sets her off. The other day I didn't load the dishwasher the way she thought it should be. So, for 15 minutes, I had to listen to her screaming and yelling about how she is the only one around here who knows how to do things the right way."

Is Name Calling Verbal Abuse?

No, you are not wrong. Your wife is verbally abusing you. Name calling hurts, belittles or puts another person is a form of verbal abuse.

Using Threats to Intimidate

When someone uses threats to intimidate they are attempting to break your will and take your power away from you. The intimidator tries to create fear in their victim. This is a form of covert abuse. There is no physical violence, just words meant to destroy you psychologically.

Using Hurtful Words to Shame

When a spouse uses hurtful words to shame we feel invalidated, disrespected and diminished. If your spouse is using words to shame you, he/she is attempting to dominate you and more than likely you are internalizing and believing the things your spouse says.

Verbal Manipulation as Abuse

When your spouse communicates with you, what is the goal of his/her communication? When married to a verbal abuser the goal is usually to gain control over you. The objective is to put you in the role of someone who meets his/her needs.

Tell Your Story of Verbal Abuse

A master at verbal abuse can damage your self-esteem while, at the same time, appear to care deeply for you. The use of words to punish is a covert attempt to control and regardless of how loving your spouse may appear, verbal abuse is wrong and can be just has harmful as physical abuse.

Using The Family Court System to Abuse a Spouse

According to Dr. Huffer, "legal abuse syndrome (LAS) is a form of posttraumatic stress disorder (PTSD). It is a psychic injury, not a mental illness. It is a personal injury that develops in individuals assaulted by ethical violations, legal abuses, betrayals, and fraud. Abuse of power and authority and a profound lack of accountability in...

Stonewalling in Marriage Relationships

Men are more prone to stonewall in a relationship because they feel overwhelmed when a wife wants to "talk feelings" or "discuss problems." We often hear men accuse their wives of "nagging" which, more often than not is in response to their stonewalling her and her need to discuss marital problems.

What Verbal Abuse is NOT

Verbal abuse is a common component of domestic violence that may occur alone or alongside physical abuse. While verbal abuse does not cause the objective scarring left by physical abuse, its emotional effects are the same. The victims frequently suffer from depression, anxiety, post-traumatic stress disorder and low self-esteem; these effects may persist for years or decades.

Some cases of verbal abuse are obvious, so most people have a vague idea of how to identify it. A person who yells, screams and curses at his partner or child-- particularly over minor affairs-- is most certainly engaging in verbal abuse. But we trivialize the extreme psychological effects of verbal abuse by applying the label too liberally.

Let's take a look at what is NOT verbal abuse.

Verbal abuse is NOT occasionally scolding or criticizing.

If your partner or parent criticizes everything you do-- from the way you walk to the way you wear your hair-- you may be a victim of verbal abuse. Constant ridiculing is a hallmark of abusive behavior. But a parent who scolds her child for consistently being late to dinner is not abusive; she's doing her job of setting order in the home. Parents and children can work together to establish a discipline method that may be less hurtful to all involved.

Types of Domestic Violence

In an equitable romantic relationship, there is far less room for criticism or scolding. But a partner who criticizes her lover's excessive drinking is not necessarily abusive. Marital feedback like "Your perfume makes me sneeze" and "please clean up after yourself in the kitchen" does not generally constitute verbal abuse.

So when is criticism the same as abuse? When it is accompanied by yelling, raging, name-calling, threats, insults or physical violence.

Verbal abuse is NOT occasionally using expletives.

Many people find expletives, or curse words, distasteful under all circumstances. In some cases, expletives may be a component of verbal abuse. However, there is a key difference between cursing at someone and cursing in front of someone. "You are a ___ing ___!" is clearly verbal abuse; it involves deliberate insult and hurtful name-calling. The extensive use of targeted expletives is a common component of violent verbal abuse.

However, "Oh ___! I left the oven on!"-- while distasteful-- would not be considered verbal abuse under most circumstances. In these cases, the target of the curse word is a situation, not a person-- the goal of the statement is to express general frustration, not cause emotional injury to another individual. In these cases, the person may benefit from finding more productive ways to vent his frustration, but he is not engaged in verbal abuse.

Verbal abuse is NOT occasionally losing one's temper.

Arguments happen. Disagreements escalate. People raise their voices. All people say things that they later regret. "Sometimes I wish we never met!" and "I hate being around you right now!" may be hurtful, but they do not generally constitute verbal abuse. If a spouse or parent says these things frequently-- particularly without qualifiers like "sometimes" and "right now"-- he may be engaged in abusive behavior. A person can say something that he later regrets without it constituting verbal abuse.

There are better ways to give feedback to a spouse or child than resorting to insulting words like "stupid" and "crazy". However, "You're acting stupid," while hurtful, is not as abusive as "You ARE stupid." A person is also not engaged in abuse if he accepts his own responsibility in familial struggles. A spouse who says "I sometimes have difficulty with my libido" is far kinder-- and more honest-- than one who tells his partner "You're unattractive."

If you're concerned that you may be the victim of verbal abuse-- or that you may be abuser-- the first step you should take is to seek counseling. A qualified relationship counselor may help to ease bumps in the relationship. Personal therapy can also help to address the emotional trauma that leads to, or results from, prolonged verbal abuse.

Visit a verbal abuse support website for more help.

Source: voices.yahoo.com/what-verbal-abuse-not-5916776.html

Physical abuse and domestic violence

When people talk about domestic violence, they are often referring to the physical abuse of a spouse or intimate partner. Physical abuse is the use of physical force against someone in a way that injures or endangers that person. Physical assault or battering is a crime, whether it occurs inside or outside of the family. The police have the power and authority to protect you from physical attack.

Sexual abuse is a form of physical abuse

Any situation in which you are forced to participate in unwanted, unsafe, or degrading sexual activity is sexual abuse. Forced sex, even by a spouse or intimate partner with whom you also have consensual sex, is an act of aggression and violence. Furthermore, people whose partners abuse them physically *and* sexually are at a higher risk of being seriously injured or killed.

It Is Still Abuse If . . .

- **The incidents of physical abuse seem minor** when compared to those you have read about, seen on television or heard other women talk about. There isn't a "better" or "worse" form of physical abuse; you can be severely injured as a result of being pushed, for example.

- **The incidents of physical abuse have only occurred one or two times in the relationship.** Studies indicate that if your spouse/partner has injured you once, it is likely he will continue to physically assault you.

- **The physical assaults stopped when you became passive** and gave up your right to express yourself as you desire, to move about freely and see others, and to make decisions. It is not a victory if you have to give up your rights as a person and a partner in exchange for not being assaulted!

Types of Domestic Violence

- **There has not been any physical violence.** Many women are emotionally and verbally assaulted. This can be as equally frightening and is often more confusing to try to understand.

Source: *Breaking the Silence: a Handbook for Victims of Violence in Nebraska*

Speak up if you suspect domestic violence or abuse

If you suspect that someone you know is being abused, speak up! If you're hesitating—telling yourself that it's none of your business, you might be wrong, or the person might not want to talk about it—keep in mind that expressing your concern will let the person know that you care and may even save his or her life.

Types of Domestic Violence

Prevention

Asoral Publishing
99

Types of Domestic Violence

Do's and Don'ts

Do:

- Ask if something is wrong
- Express concern
- Listen and validate
- Offer help
- Support his or her decisions

Don't:

- Wait for him or her to come to you
- Judge or blame
- Pressure him or her
- Give advice
- Place conditions on your support

Types of Domestic Violence

Adapted from: *NYS Office for the Prevention of Domestic Violence*

Talk to the person in private and let him or her know that you're concerned. Point out the things you've noticed that make you worried. Tell the person that you're there, whenever he or she feels ready to talk. Reassure the person that you'll keep whatever is said between the two of you, and let him or her know that you'll help in any way you can.

Remember, abusers are very good at controlling and manipulating their victims. People who have been emotionally abused or battered are depressed, drained, scared, ashamed, and confused. They need help to get out, yet they've often been isolated from their family and friends. By picking up on the warning signs and offering support, you can help them escape an abusive situation and begin healing.

Getting out of an abusive relationship.

Do you want to leave an abusive situation, but stay out of fear of what your partner might do? While leaving isn't easy, there are things you can do to protect yourself. You're not alone, and help is available for abused and battered women.

DOMESTIC VIOLENCE PREVENTION

What Can Each of Us Do To Prevent Domestic Violence?

- Call the police if you see or hear evidence of domestic violence.
- Speak out publicly against domestic violence.
- Take action personally against domestic violence when a neighbor, a co-worker, a friend, or a family member is involved or being abused.
- Encourage your neighborhood watch or block association to become as concerned with watching out for domestic violence as with burglaries and other crimes.
- Reach out to support someone whom you believe is a victim of domestic violence and/or talk with a person you believe is being abusive.

Types of Domestic Violence

- Help others become informed, by inviting speakers to your church, professional organization, civic group, or workplace.
- Support domestic violence counseling programs and shelters.

Emotional abuse: It's a bigger problem than you think

When people think of domestic abuse, they often picture battered women who have been physically assaulted. But not all abusive relationships involve violence. Just because you're not battered and bruised doesn't mean you're not being abused. Many men and women suffer from emotional abuse, which is no less destructive. Unfortunately, emotional abuse is often minimized or overlooked—even by the person being abused.

Understanding emotional abuse

The aim of emotional abuse is to chip away at your feelings of self-worth and independence. If you're the victim of emotional abuse, you may feel that there is no way out of the relationship or that without your abusive partner you have nothing.

Emotional abuse includes *verbal abuse* such as yelling, name-calling, blaming, and shaming. Isolation, intimidation, and controlling behavior also fall under emotional abuse. Additionally, abusers who use emotional or psychological abuse often throw in threats of physical violence or other repercussions if you don't do what they want.

You may think that physical abuse is far worse than emotional abuse, since physical violence can send you to the hospital and leave you with scars. But, the scars of emotional abuse are very real, and they run deep. In fact, emotional abuse can be just as damaging as physical abuse—sometimes even more so.

Economic or financial abuse: A subtle form of emotional abuse

Remember, an abuser's goal is to control you, and he or she will frequently use money to do so. Economic or financial abuse includes:

- Rigidly controlling your finances

- Withholding money or credit cards

- Making you account for every penny you spend

- Withholding basic necessities (food, clothes, medications, shelter)

- Restricting you to an allowance

- Preventing you from working or choosing your own career

- Sabotaging your job (making you miss work, calling constantly)

- Stealing from you or taking your money

Types of Domestic Violence

Violent and abusive behavior is the abuser's choice

Despite what many people believe, domestic violence and abuse is not due to the abuser's loss of control over his or her behavior. In fact, abusive behavior and violence is a deliberate choice made by the abuser in order to control you.

Abusers use a variety of tactics to manipulate you and exert their power:

- **Dominance** – Abusive individuals need to feel in charge of the relationship. They will make decisions for you and the family, tell you what to do, and expect you to obey without question. Your abuser may treat you like a servant, child, or even as his or her possession.

- **Humiliation** – An abuser will do everything he or she can to make you feel bad about yourself or defective in some way. After all, if you believe you're worthless and that no one else will want you, you're less likely to

Types of Domestic Violence

leave. Insults, name-calling, shaming, and public put-downs are all weapons of abuse designed to erode your self-esteem and make you feel powerless.

- **Isolation** – In order to increase your dependence on him or her, an abusive partner will cut you off from the outside world. He or she may keep you from seeing family or friends, or even prevent you from going to work or school. You may have to ask permission to do anything, go anywhere, or see anyone.

- **Threats** – Abusers commonly use threats to keep their partners from leaving or to scare them into dropping charges. Your abuser may threaten to hurt or kill you, your children, other family members, or even pets. He or she may also threaten to commit suicide, file false charges against you, or report you to child services.

- **Intimidation** – Your abuser may use a variety of intimidation tactics designed to

Types of Domestic Violence

scare you into submission. Such tactics include making threatening looks or gestures, smashing things in front of you, destroying property, hurting your pets, or putting weapons on display. The clear message is that if you don't obey, there will be violent consequences.

- **Denial and blame** – Abusers are very good at making excuses for the inexcusable. They will blame their abusive and violent behavior on a bad childhood, a bad day, and even on the victims of their abuse. Your abusive partner may minimize the abuse or deny that it occurred. He or she will commonly shift the responsibility on to you: Somehow, his or her violent and abusive behavior is your fault.

Abusers *are* able to control their behavior—they do it all the time

- **Abusers pick and choose whom to abuse.** They don't insult, threaten, or assault everyone in their life who gives them grief.

Usually, they save their abuse for the people closest to them, the ones they claim to love.

- **Abusers carefully choose when and where to abuse.** They control themselves until no one else is around to see their abusive behavior. They may act like everything is fine in public, but lash out instantly as soon as you're alone.

- **Abusers are able to stop their abusive behavior when it benefits them.** Most abusers are not out of control. In fact, they're able to immediately stop their abusive behavior when it's to their advantage to do so (for example, when the police show up or their boss calls).

- **Violent abusers usually direct their blows where they won't show.** Rather than acting out in a mindless rage, many physically violent abusers carefully aim their kicks and punches where the bruises and marks won't show.

Types of Domestic Violence

The cycle of violence in domestic abuse

Domestic abuse falls into a common pattern, or cycle of violence:

- **Abuse** – Your abusive partner lashes out with aggressive, belittling, or violent behavior. The abuse is a power play designed to show you "who is boss."

Types of Domestic Violence

- **Guilt** – After abusing you, your partner feels guilt, but not over what he's done. He's more worried about the possibility of being caught and facing consequences for his abusive behavior

- **Excuses** – Your abuser rationalizes what he or she has done. The person may come up with a string of excuses or blame you for the abusive behavior—anything to avoid taking responsibility.

- **"Normal" behavior** – The abuser does everything he can to regain control and keep the victim in the relationship. He may act as if nothing has happened, or he may turn on the charm. This peaceful honeymoon phase may give the victim hope that the abuser has really changed this time.

Types of Domestic Violence

- **Fantasy and planning** – Your abuser begins to fantasize about abusing you again. He spends a lot of time thinking about what you've done wrong and how he'll make you pay. Then he makes a plan for turning the fantasy of abuse into reality.

- **Set-up** – Your abuser sets you up and puts his plan in motion, creating a situation where he can justify abusing you.

Your abuser's apologies and loving gestures in between the episodes of abuse can make it difficult to leave. He may make you believe that you are the only person who can help him, that things will be different this time, and that he truly loves you. However, the dangers of staying are very real.

Types of Domestic Violence

The Full Cycle of Domestic Violence: An Example

A man **abuses** his partner. After he hits her, he experiences self-directed **guilt**. He says, "I'm sorry for hurting you." What he does not say is, "Because I might get caught." He then **rationalizes** his behavior by saying that his partner is having an affair with someone. He tells her "If you weren't such a worthless whore I wouldn't have to hit you." He then **acts contrite**, reassuring her that he will not hurt her again. He then **fantasizes** and reflects on past abuse and how he will hurt her again. He **plans** on telling her to go to the store to get some groceries. What he withholds from her is that she has a certain amount of time to do the shopping. When she is held up in traffic and is a few minutes late, he feels completely justified in assaulting her because "you're having an affair with the store clerk." He has just **set her up**.

Source: *Mid-Valley Women's Crisis Service*

National Resources

Asoral Publishing

National Resource Center on Domestic Violence

1-800-799-7233 (SAFE)
TTY 1-800-787-3224

MISSION

As part of a social change movement to end gender based violence, the NRCDV engages with and learns from, informs and supports systems, organizations, communities, and individuals to strengthen capacity to effectively address domestic violence and intersecting issues.

VISION

The NRCDV strives to be a trusted national leader and sustainable organization, renowned for innovation, multi-disciplinary approaches and a commitment to ensuring that policy, practice and research is grounded in and guided by the voices and experiences of domestic violence survivors and advocates.

BRIEF ORGANIZATIONAL HISTORY

After being established in 1993 with funding from the U.S. Department of Health and Human Services (HHS), the National Resource Center on Domestic Violence operated as a national project housed

Resources

within the structure of the Pennsylvania Coalition Against Domestic Violence (PCADV), one of the first and most respected state coalitions. Working closely with an expert resource center staff, PCADV carefully nurtured the growth and development of the resource center. In late 2011, after discussions with key stakeholders (other domestic violence coalitions, national partners, consultants, funders, and NRCDV staff) and a thoughtful assessment, the National Resource Center on Domestic Violence, Inc. (NRCDV) was formed as an independent non-profit organization to carry on this work.

The National Resource Center on Domestic Violence provides a wide range of free, comprehensive, and individualized technical assistance, training, and specialized resource materials and key initiatives designed to enhance current domestic violence intervention and prevention strategies. Reach the NRCDV Technical Assistance Specialist for guidance at 1-800-537-2238 / TTY 1-800-553-2508 or via email at nrcdvTA@nrcdv.org. Or complete the NRCDV Online TA request form.

Resources

National Dating Abuse Hotline

1-866-331-9474
TTY 1-866-331-8453
Text "loveis" to 22522

About loveisrespect.org

Break the Cycle and the National Dating Abuse Helpline are collaborating to bring you loveisrespect.org. By combining our resources and capacity, we are reaching more people, building more healthy relationships and saving more lives.

We designed loveisrespect.org to:

Create the ultimate resource fostering healthy dating attitudes and relationships.

Provide a safe space for young people to access information and help in an environment that is designed specifically for them.

Ensure confidentiality and trust so young people feel safe and supported—online and off.

We are proud to call loveisrespect.org the ultimate resource to engage, educate and empower youth and young adults to prevent and end abusive relationships.

Break the Cycle

Asoral Publishing

Resources

Break the Cycle is the leading voice dedicated to the prevention of dating abuse. Learn more about our services and resources available nationwide.

National Dating Abuse Helpline

The National Dating Abuse Helpline is a program of the National Council on Family Violence. Learn more about our work and the advocates who assist young people 24/7.

Our National Advisory Board

Find out more about the national advisers working to make sure loveisrespect.org is the most comprehensive resource for young people on the issue of dating abuse.

Our National Youth Advisory Board

Find out more about the young people who are making sure loveisrespect.org provides the most youth-friendly and highest-quality resources and services available.

Resources

The Rape Abuse Incest National Network

1-800-656-4673 (HOPE)

Mission Statement

RAINN (Rape, Abuse & Incest National Network) is the nation's largest anti-sexual violence organization and was named one of "America's 100 Best Charities" by Worth magazine. RAINN created and operates the National Sexual Assault Hotline (800.656.HOPE and online.rainn.org) in partnership with more than 1,100 local rape crisis centers across the country and operates the DoD Safe Helpline for the Department of Defense. RAINN also carries out programs to prevent sexual violence, help victims and ensure that rapists are brought to justice.

Resources

National Online Resource Center on Violence Against Women

'A project of the National Resource Center on Domestic Violence'.

Our resource library is home to thousands of materials on violence against women and related issues, with particular attention to its intersections with various forms of oppression.

Here you'll find resources on domestic violence, sexual violence, funding, research, and international issues. You'll also find news, announcements, and events related to the work of the movement and related fields of practice. From the comprehensive lists of resources found in Special Collections to the concise interpretations of current research in our peer-reviewed Applied Research Papers, VAWnet has a variety of formats and material types to offer. For tips on navigating or searching the library, see How to Use VAWnet.org.

VAWnet supports local, state, and national prevention and intervention strategies that enhance safety and well-being and address the self-identified needs and concerns of victims and survivors. To learn more, visit About VAWnet.

Resources

National Indigenous Women's Resource Center

406.477.3896
or Toll-Free: 855.649.7299 (855.NIWRC99)
www.niwrc.org/partner-collaboration/dvrn

The National Indigenous Women's Resource Center, Inc. (NIWRC) is a Native nonprofit organization that was created specifically to serve as the National Indian Resource Center (NIRC) Addressing Domestic Violence and Safety for Indian Women. Under this grant project and in compliance with statutory requirements, the NIWRC will seek to enhance the capacity of American Indian and Alaska Native (Native) tribes, Native Hawaiians, and Tribal and Native Hawaiian organizations to respond to domestic violence.

The NIWRC, through its Board of Directors and staff, have the demonstrated and unique expertise to serve as the next National Indian Resource Center. Our Board consists of Native women from throughout the United States with extensive experience and commitment to providing technical assistance/training and resource information regarding violence committed against Native women and their children. This leadership will ensure that our work supports and upholds

Resources

grassroots advocacy and policy development work to address these crimes. Further, the NIWRC's staff brings decades of expertise, regarding violence against Native women, each of us having worked in various capacities to build a strong grassroots movement to increase the response within tribes to domestic violence and safety for Indian.

The NIWRC is dedicated to reclaiming the sovereignty of Native nations and safeguarding Native women and their children. Through public awareness and resource development, training and technical assistance, policy development, and research activities, we will provide leadership across the Nation to show that offenders can and will be held accountable and that Native women and their children are entitled to: 1) safety from violence within their homes and in their community; 2) justice both on and off tribal lands; and 3) access to services designed by and for Native women based on their tribal beliefs and practices.

Asoral Publishing

Resources

National Sexual Assault Hotline

1.800.656.HOPE(4673) | Free. Confidential. 24/7.

Among its programs, RAINN created and operates the National Sexual Assault Hotline at 1.800.656.HOPE. This nationwide partnership of more than 1,100 local rape treatment hotlines provides victims of sexual violence with free, confidential services around the clock. The hotline helped 137,039 sexual assault victims in 2005 and has helped more than 1.5 million since it began in 1994.

Resources

National Network to end Domestic Violence

1-800-799-SAFE (7233)
1-800-787-3224 (TTY)

1400 16th St NW, Suite 330
Washington, DC 20036
phone: 202-543-5566
fax: 202-543-5626

The National Network to End Domestic Violence (NNEDV), a social change organization, is dedicated to creating a social, political and economic environment in which violence against women no longer exists.

Making domestic violence a national priority.

NNEDV is the leading voice for domestic violence victims and their advocates. As a membership and advocacy organization of state domestic violence coalitions, allied organizations and supportive individuals, NNEDV works closely with its members to understand the ongoing and emerging needs of domestic violence victims and advocacy programs. Then NNEDV makes sure those needs are heard and understood by policymakers at the national level.

Changing the way society responds to domestic violence.

NNEDV offers a range of programs and initiatives to address the complex causes and far-reaching consequences of domestic violence. Through cross-sector collaborations and corporate partnerships, NNEDV offers support to victims of domestic violence who are escaping abusive relationships – and empowers survivors to build new lives.

Strengthening domestic violence advocacy at every level.

NNEDV further supports the fight to end domestic violence by providing state coalitions with critical information and resources. From training and technical assistance to innovative programs and strategic funding, NNEDV brings much-needed resources to local communities. At NNEDV's national and regional meetings, members share information and ideas with NNEDV staff and with each other, working together to develop comprehensive solutions.

Resources

Safe Horizon

Safe Horizon moves victims of violence from crisis to confidence 1-800-621-4673 or 1-800-621-HOPE.

Safe Horizon is the nation's leading victim assistance organization. Our mission is to provide support, prevent violence, and promote justice for victims of crime and abuse, their families and communities. Our 57 programs are located throughout the five boroughs of New York City in court houses, police precincts, schools, shelters, and community offices. Safe Horizon's first priority is the safety of those who seek assistance. Our programs work with clients to meet their needs so they can look ahead to a safe horizon.

Providing 24-Hour Lifelines to Crime Victims

Safe Horizon's four toll-free hotlines are gateways to assistance for more than 250,000 of the city's crime victims each year. The state-of-the art program is staffed by experienced professionals 24 hours a day, seven days a week including holidays. Many hotline advocates are multilingual, and all counselors are able to utilize a translation service to assist callers who speak a language not represented. Hotline advocates provide crisis counseling, safety planning, assistance with finding shelter, referrals to

Resources

Safe Horizon programs or other organizations, advocacy with the police, and other crucial services.

Hotlines

Safe Horizon's Domestic Violence Hotline:
800.621.HOPE (4673)
Safe Horizon's Crime Victims Hotline:
866.689.HELP (4357)
Safe Horizon's Rape, Sexual Assault & Incest Hotline:
212.227.3000

TDD phone number for all hotlines:
866.604.5350
Our Hotline staff

- Keeps your information confidential and private.

- Can help you with safety planning.

- Can offer referrals to counseling, legal services, housing, and other support.

Resources

Futures Without Violence

Everyone has the right to live free of violence.

Under the leadership and vision of founder Esta Soler for more than 30 years, Futures Without Violence has led the way and set the pace for ground-breaking education programs, national policy development, professional training programs, and public actions designed to end violence against women, children and families around the world. In 1994, Futures Without Violence was instrumental in developing the landmark Violence Against Women Act passed by the U.S. Congress.

Providing leadership from offices in San Francisco, Washington D.C. and Boston, we have established a state-of-the-art Center for Leadership and Action in the Presidio of San Francisco to foster ongoing dialogue about gender-based violence and child abuse. Striving to reach new audiences and transform social norms, we train professionals such as doctors, nurses, athletic coaches, and judges on improving responses to violence and abuse. We also work with advocates, policy makers and others to build sustainable community leadership and educate people everywhere about the importance of respect and healthy relationships.

Resources

To learn more about what has driven us for over thirty years, get the facts about the prevalence and devastating effects of violence.

Main Office
Futures Without Violence
100 Montgomery Street, The Presidio
San Francisco, CA 94129
Phone: (415) 678-5500
Fax: (415) 529-2930
TTY: (800) 595-4889
Driving Directions

Washington, DC Office
1320 19th St. NW
Suite 401
Washington, D.C. 20036
Phone: (202) 595-7382
Fax: (202) 299-1292

Boston, MA Office
281 Summer Street
5th Floor
Boston, MA 02210
Phone: (617) 702-2004
Fax: (617) 426-0748

Asoral Publishing

Resources

The Children's Aid Society

(212) 503-6842

Domestic Violence Prevention and Intervention Services

The Children's Aid Society believes that when there is violence in the home, every member of the family is affected. That's why the Family Wellness Program addresses domestic violence from the perspective of the entire family.

A wide range of services is available for those who have experienced violence in their homes or in dating relationships. They include:

- Individual counseling for survivors of abuse, and children and teens who have witnessed abuse.
- Family counseling for children and their non-abusive parents.
- Group counseling for women, children and teens.
- Men's groups for men who have used abusive behavior in intimate relationships.
- Case management and advocacy services, including help acquiring public assistance, orders of protection, housing and shelter as

Resources

well as referrals for other services when necessary.
Services are provided free-of-cost in English and Spanish at several locations in Manhattan and the Bronx.

Resources

Family and Youth Services Bureau

The Domestic Violence Resource Network (DVRN) is funded by the U.S. Department of Health and Human Services to inform and strengthen domestic violence intervention and prevention efforts at the individual, community and societal levels.

The DVRN works collaboratively to promote practices and strategies to improve our nation's response to domestic violence and make safety and justice not just a priority, but also a reality. DVRN member agencies ensure that victims of domestic violence, advocates, community-based programs, educators, legal assistance providers, law enforcement and court personnel, health care providers, policy makers and government leaders at the local, state, tribal and federal levels have access to up--to--date information on best practices, policies, research and victim resources.

The DVRN includes two national resource centers, four special issue resource centers, three culturally--specific Institutes, and the National Domestic Violence Hotline.

What We Do

The mission of the Family and Youth Services Bureau (FYSB) is to promote safety, stability, and

Resources

well-being for people who have experienced or been exposed to violence, neglect or trauma. FYSB achieves this through supporting programs that provide shelter, community services and prevention education for youth, adults and families.

FYSB is made up of two divisions that house three major grant programs:

Division of Adolescent Development and Support

- Runaway and Homeless Youth Program
- Adolescent Pregnancy Prevention Program

Division of Family Violence Prevention and Services

- Family Violence Prevention and Services Program

In addition, we support nationwide crisis hotlines for runaway youth and victims of domestic violence.

Help for Runaway and Homeless Youth
National Runaway Safeline
1-800-RUNAWAY (786-2929)

National Clearinghouse on Families & Youth
(301) 608-8098

Resources

Help for Victims and Survivors of Domestic Violence

National Domestic Violence Hotline
1-800-799-SAFE (1-800-799-7223)
TTY: (800) 787-3244
Free and confidential help is available for victims of domestic violence 24 hours a day. If you need help or just want someone to talk to, please call the National Domestic Violence Hotline at: 1-800-799-SAFE (7233) or TTY 1-800-787-3224. As a survivor of domestic violence, your safety is at high risk when you leave an abusive relationship and right after you make that decision. It is important to work with a domestic violence advocate to develop a safety plan. Advocates can help you develop a plan for emergencies, connect you to community resources and discuss your options.

National Resource Center on Domestic Violence
(800) 537-2238

National Indigenous Women's Resource Center
(855) 649-7299

Battered Women's Justice Project Criminal and Civil Justice Center & National Clearinghouse for the Defense of Battered Women

Asoral Publishing

Resources

(800) 903-0111

National Health Resource Center on Domestic Violence
(888) 792-2873

National Center on Domestic Violence, Trauma & Mental Health
(312) 726-7020

Resource Center on Domestic Violence: Child Protection and Custody
(800) 527-3223

Asian & Pacific Islander Institute on Domestic Violence
(415) 568-3315

Casa de Esperanza: National Latin@ Network of Healthy Families and Communities
(651) 646-5553

Institute on Domestic Violence in the African American Community
(877) 643-8222

Expanding Services for Children & Youth Exposed DV Technical Assistance Futures Without Violence Children's Program
(617) 426-8667

Resources

Help for Victims of Human Trafficking and Commercial Sexual Exploitation

National Human Trafficking Resource Center
1-888-373-7888
or text HELP or INFO to BeFree (233733)

Safety Tips

Domestic Violence Safety Tips
If you are in immediate danger, please:

Call 911.
Call your local hotline.
Call a national hotline.

- Call the U.S. National Domestic Violence Hotline: 1-800-799-7233 (SAFE) or TTY 1-800-787-3224.
- Call, text or chat Love Is Respect—The National Teen Dating Abuse Helpline: 1-866-331-9474 or TTY 1-866-331-8453, text "loveis" to 22522 or live chat at www.loveisrespect.org.
- Call the U.S. National Sexual Assault Hotline: 1-800-656-4673 (HOPE), which

Resources

automatically connects you to a local U.S. rape crisis program based on the area code of your phone number. Secure, online private chat is available at **ohl.rainn.org/online/**.

Remember: Corded phones are more private and less able to be intercepted than cordless phones or analog cell phones.

Be Aware: You may not be able to reach 911 using an Internet phone or Internet-based phone service. So you may need to be prepared to use another phone to call 911.

Contact your local domestic violence program, shelter, or rape crisis center to learn about free cell phone donation programs.

Tips for Using Technology

If you think your activities are being monitored, they probably are.
Abusive people are often controlling and want to know your every move. You don't need to be a computer programmer or have special skills to monitor someone's computer and Internet activities. Anyone can do it and there are many ways to monitor with programs like Spyware, keystroke loggers and hacking tools.

Resources

It is not possible to delete or clear all the "footprints" of your computer or online activities.
If you are being monitored, it may be dangerous to change your computer behaviors such as suddenly deleting your entire Internet history if that is not your regular habit.

If you think you may be monitored on your home computer, be careful how you use your computer since an abuser might become suspicious.
You may want to keep using the monitored computer for innocuous activities, like looking up the weather. Use a safer computer to research an escape plan, look for new jobs or apartments, bus tickets, or ask for help.

Email and Instant/Text Messaging (IM) are not safe or confidential ways to talk to someone about the danger or abuse in your life.
If possible, please call a hotline instead. If you use email or IM, please use a safer computer and an account your abuser does not know about.

Computers can store a lot of private information.
This includes what you look at via the Internet, the emails and instant messages you send, internet-based phone and IP-TTY calls you make, web-

Resources

based purchases and banking, and many other activities.

It might be safer to use a computer in a public library, at a community technology center (CTC) at a trusted friends house, or an Internet Cafe.

Modern technology and social networks change frequently. Educate yourself by reading about the NRCDV's Tech Safety Resources. This special collection of selected articles, fact sheets, papers, reports and other materials are designed to assist advocates and survivors interested in understanding the safe use of technology.

Source (National Resource Center on Domestic Violence)

Myths and Facts about Domestic Violence

MYTH #1: DOMESTIC VIOLENCE AFFECTS ONLY A SMALL PERCENTAGE OF THE POPULATION AND IS RARE.

FACT: National studies estimate that 3 to 4 million women are beaten each year in our country. A study conducted in 1995 found that 31% of women surveyed admitted to having been physically assaulted by a husband or boyfriend. Domestic violence is the leading cause of injury to women between the ages of 15 and 44 in our country, and the FBI estimates that a woman is beaten every 15 seconds. Thirty percent of female homicide victims are killed by partners or ex-partners and 1,500 women are murdered as a result of domestic violence each year in the United States.

MYTH #2: DOMESTIC VIOLENCE OCCURS ONLY IN POOR, UNEDUCATED AND MINORITY FAMILIES.

FACT: Studies of domestic violence consistently have found that battering occurs among all types of families, regardless of income, profession, region, ethnicity, educational level or race. However, the fact that lower income victims and abusers are over-represented in calls to police, battered women's shelters and social services may be due to a lack of other resources.

MYTH #3: THE REAL PROBLEM IS COUPLES WHO ASSAULT EACH OTHER. WOMEN ARE JUST AS VIOLENT AS MEN.

FACT: A well-publicized study conducted by Dr. Murray Strauss at the University of New Hampshire found that women use violent means to resolve conflict in relationships as often as men. However, the study also concluded that when the context and consequences of an assault are measured, the majority of victims are women. The U.S. Department of Justice has found that 85% of the victims of spouse abuse are female. Men can be victims, but it is rare.

MYTH #4: ALCOHOL ABUSE CAUSES DOMESTIC VIOLENCE.

FACT: Although there is a high correlation between alcohol, or other substance abuse, and battering, it is not a causal relationship. Batterers use drinking as one of many excuses for their violence and as a way to place the responsibility for their violence elsewhere. Stopping the abusers' drinking will not stop the violence. Both battering and substance abuse need to be addressed separately, as overlapping yet independent problems.

MYTH #5: DOMESTIC VIOLENCE IS USUALLY A ONE TIME, ISOLATED OCCURRENCE.

FACT: Battering is a pattern of coercion and control that one person exerts over another. Battering is not just one physical attack. It includes the repeated use of a number of tactics, including intimidation, threats, economic deprivation, isolation and psychological and sexual abuse. Physical violence is just one of these tactics. The various forms of abuse utilized by batterers help to maintain power and control over their spouses and partners.

MYTH #6: MEN WHO BATTER ARE OFTEN GOOD FATHERS AND SHOULD HAVE JOINT CUSTODY OF THEIR CHILDREN IF THE COUPLE SEPARATES.

Fact: Studies have found that men who batter their wives also abuse their children in 70% of cases. Even when children are not directly abused, they suffer as a result of witnessing one parent assault another. Batterers often display an increased interest in their children at the time of separation, as a means of maintaining contact with, and thus control over, their partners.

MYTH #7: WHEN THERE IS VIOLENCE IN THE FAMILY, ALL MEMBERS OF THE FAMILY ARE PARTICIPATING IN THE DYNAMIC, AND THEREFORE, ALL MUST CHANGE FOR THE VIOLENCE TO STOP.

FACT: Only the batterer has the ability to stop the violence. Battering is a behavioral choice for which the batterer must be held accountable. Many battered women make numerous attempts to change their behavior in the hope that this will stop the abuse. This does not work. Changes in family members' behavior will not cause the batterer to be non-violent.

MYTH #8: BATTERED WOMEN ARE MASOCHISTIC AND PROVOKE THE ABUSE. THEY MUST LIKE IT OR THEY WOULD LEAVE.

FACT: Victim provocation is no more common in domestic violence than in any other crime. Battered women often make repeated attempts to leave violent relationships, but are prevented from doing so by increased violence and control tactics on the part of the abuser. Other factors which inhibit a victim's ability to leave include economic dependence, few viable options for housing and support, unhelpful responses from the criminal justice system or other agencies, social isolation, cultural or religious constraints, a commitment to the abuser and the relationship and fear of further violence. It has been estimated that the danger to a victim increases by 70% when she attempts to leave, as the abuser escalates his use of violence when he begins to lose control.

MYTH #9: MEN HAVE A RIGHT TO DISCIPLINE THEIR PARTNERS FOR MISBEHAVING. BATTERING IS NOT A CRIME.

FACT: While our society derives from a patriarchal legal system that afforded men the right to physically chastise their wives and children, we do not live under such a system now. Women and children are no longer considered the property of men, and domestic violence is a crime in every state in the country.

Source:clarkcountyprosecutor.org

Family Violence

Family violence is the physical, sexual and/or psychological coercion to establish and maintain control.

SIGNS AND SYMPTOMS

- If a spouse, partner, family member, or caretaker:
- Hits, slaps, punches, chokes kick, pushes, shoves, or spits on you
- Threatens or scares you with a weapon
- Forces or coerces you to have sex when you don't want to
- Threatens to take your children away
- Blames you for his/her violent behavior
- Withholds affection as punishment
- Takes away your house keys, car keys, or money
- Keeps you from seeking medical attention
- Says that you deserve to be hit
- Tries to isolate you from your family and friends

You may be a victim of Family Violence

How to identify if someone you know may be a victim.

Family Violence

Warning signs may be indications of various problems, but some indicators that someone may be the victim of Domestic Violence include:

- Unexplained bruises
- Lack of concentration
- Change of work performance or attitude
- Receipt of harassing phone calls
- Disruptive personal visits to the workplace
- Depression and anxiety

Domestic violence Against Men

Domestic violence against men isn't always easy to identify, but it can be a serious threat. Know how to recognize if you're being abused — and how to get help.

Women aren't the only victims of domestic violence. Understand the signs of domestic violence against men, and know how to get help.

Recognize domestic violence against men

Domestic violence — also known as domestic abuse, battering or intimate partner violence — occurs between people in an intimate relationship. Domestic violence against men can take many forms, including emotional, sexual and physical abuse and threats of abuse. It can happen in heterosexual or same sex relationships.

It might not be easy to recognize domestic violence against men. Early in the relationship, your partner might seem attentive, generous and protective in ways that later turn out to be controlling and frightening. Initially, the abuse might appear as isolated incidents. Your partner might apologize and promise not to abuse you again.

In other relationships, domestic violence against men might include both partners slapping or shoving each other when they get angry — and neither partner seeing himself or herself as being abused or controlled. This type of violence, however, can still devastate a relationship, causing both physical and emotional damage.

You might be experiencing domestic violence if your partner:

- Calls you names, insults you or puts you down

- Prevents you from going to work or school

- Stops you from seeing family members or friends

- Tries to control how you spend money, where you go or what you wear

- Acts jealous or possessive or constantly accuses you of being unfaithful

- Gets angry when drinking alcohol or using drugs

- Threatens you with violence or a weapon

- Hits, kicks, shoves, slaps, chokes or otherwise hurts you, your children or your pets

- Assaults you while you're sleeping, you've been drinking or you're not paying attention to make up for a difference in strength

- Forces you to have sex or engage in sexual acts against your will
- Blames you for his or her violent behavior or tells you that you deserve it
- Portrays the violence as mutual and consensual

If you're gay, bisexual or transgender, you might also be experiencing domestic violence if you're in a relationship with someone who:

- Threatens to tell friends, family, colleagues or community members your sexual orientation or gender identity
- Tells you that authorities won't help a gay, bisexual or transgender person
- Tells you that leaving the relationship means you're admitting that gay, bisexual or transgender relationships are deviant
- Justifies abuse by telling you that you're not "really" gay, bisexual or transgender
- Says that men are naturally violent

Escaping Domestic Violence by Women or Domestic Partners

While the majority of domestic violence victims are women, abuse of men happens far more often than you'd probably expect. Typically, men are physically stronger than women but that doesn't necessarily make it easier to escape the violence or the relationship. An abused man faces a shortage of resources, skepticism from police, and major legal obstacles, especially when it comes to gaining custody of his children from an abusive mother. No matter your age, occupation, or sexual orientation, though, you can overcome these challenges and escape the abuse.

More than 830,000 men fall victim to domestic violence every year, which means every 37.8 seconds, somewhere in America a man is battered, according to the National Violence Against Women Survey. While more than 1.5 million women are also victims, everyone -- no matter their sex -- deserves help.

"Domestic violence is not about size, gender, or strength," says Jan Brown, executive director and founder of the Domestic Abuse Helpline for Men. "It's about abuse, control, and power, and getting out of dangerous situations and getting help, whether you are a woman being abused, or a man."

There are more than 4,000 domestic violence programs in the U.S., but Brown says very few actually offer the same services to men as they do women. So where can a man turn for support when he is being abused? Domestic violence experts offer advice for men who may be falling through the cracks.

Abuse Against Men

"Domestic violence against men is very similar to domestic violence against women," says Brown. "It can come in the form of physical abuse, emotional, verbal, or financial."

As with abuse against women, Brown explains that abuse against men can mean a partner or spouse will:

Against Men

Withhold approval, appreciation, or affection as punishment

- Criticize, name call, or shout
- Take away your car keys or money
- Regularly threaten to leave or to make you leave
- Threaten to hurt you or a family member
- Punish or deprive your children when angry at you
- Threaten to kidnap the children if you leave
- Abuse or hurt your pets
- Harass you about affairs your spouse imagines you are having
- Manipulate you with lies and contradictions
- Destroy furniture, punch holes in walls, break appliances
- Wield a gun/knife in a threatening way
- Hit, kick, shove, punch, bite, spit, or throw things when upset

In one instance, Brown received a letter from a woman who said her brother was being abused by his wife, who would scratch him, throw things at him, point a gun at him, break his eyeglasses, and flush his medications down the toilet -- among other things.

"The sister said in her letter that her brother stitched a cut on his arm himself, with a thread and needle, because his wife had cut him and he didn't want to go to the hospital," says Brown. "Can you imagine being so embarrassed that your wife hits you that you do that?"

Distinguishing Factors

That is a distinguishing factor between battered women and battered men, explains Brown: Men -- like this one -- are more likely to be embarrassed by their abuse, making them less likely to report it, according to the Domestic Abuse Helpline for Men web site, which states men often worry, "What will people think if they knew I let a woman beat up on me?" and "I don't want to be laughed at; no one would believe me."

Another distinguishing factor is that while women who are abused are more likely to be pushed or shoved, beat up, or threatened with a gun, the women who do the abusing are more likely to throw something, kick or bite, hit with an object, threaten with a knife, or actually use a knife, according to the National Violence Against Women Survey.

And perhaps the most important difference is that women who batter may have a greater ability to use the "system" to their advantage.

"Systemic abuse can occur when a woman who is abusing her husband or boyfriend threatens that he will never see his children again if he leaves or reports the abuse," says Philip Cook, program director of Stop Abuse for Everyone. "A man caught in this situation believes that no matter what his wife or girlfriend does, the court is going to give her custody, and this greatly limits his ability to leave. While this can occur when a woman is being abused, it is more likely to happen when a woman is abusing."

Women, explains Cook, who is author of *Abused Men: The Hidden Side of Domestic Violence*, may also be able to use the system to their advantage in that they are less likely to be arrested if police are called as a result of a domestic dispute.

"There is no national data on average arrest rates for women in domestic disputes," says Cook. "My best guess is that it's about 20%. But we do know anecdotally that there are many men who, when the police arrive, clearly have the most serious injury, clearly when interviewed separately indicate the female started it, and nonetheless, the man gets arrested. This does indeed happen."

So where can men who are being abused turn for support, and what steps should they take to get out of dangerous situations?

Getting Help

The first step in getting help is reaching out.

"The Domestic Abuse Helpline for Men is the only one in the nation that offers support and help in finding resources specifically for men," says Brown, of the not-for-profit helpline. "We'll provide options and support and help a man understand that the abuse is not his fault and it is not acceptable." The Domestic Abuse Helpline can be reached from anywhere in the US and Canada, 24 hours a day, seven days a week, by calling 1-888-7HELPLINE (1-888-743-5754).

"What people should know is that abuse is about power and control, and regardless of whether the victim is a man or a woman, it is never OK," says Havilah Tower-Perkins, media relations coordinator for the National Domestic Violence Hotline. "We urge anyone whose relationship scares them to call the National Domestic Violence Hotline (NDVH) at (800) 799-SAFE (7233) or the TTY line for the deaf: (800) 787-3224. The Hotline is staffed 24 hours a day, year round with live advocates who can answer questions, discuss safety options, and connect callers to resources in their local area. Every call to

Stopping the Abuse

Other steps for men who are being abused to take include:

- "Never allow yourself to be provoked into any kind of retaliation," says Brown. "We tell men if they have to be in an argument, do it in a room with two doors so they can leave; a lot of times a woman will block the door, the man will try to move her, and that will be enough for him to get arrested."

- "Document everything," says Cook. "Go to your doctor and tell him what happened, even if he doesn't ask how you were injured. Take photographs of your injuries, and make sure if the police are called that they take a report, and get a copy of the report for yourself."

- "Work with an advocate from a domestic violence program to get a restraining order," says Brown. "Not only will this help protect you from an abusive partner, but it will also allow you to ask for temporary custody of your children in order to protect them from the domestic violence."

- Get counseling so you can start healing, and get legal advice, says Cook.

- Talk with your family and friends who can help support you. "They will understand," says Brown.

"Abusers are good at making you feel isolated and alone, but you're not," says Brown. "We get calls from all types of people -- doctors, lawyers, laborers, people in the military. The biggest hurdle they face is finding someone who believes them. If they are believed, they can get help, and that's why we're here."

Why Men don't Leave

Many people have trouble understanding why a woman who is being abused by her husband or boyfriend doesn't simply just leave him. When the roles are reversed, and the man is the victim of the abuse, people are even more bemused. However, anyone who's been in an abusive relationship knows that it's never that simple. Ending a relationship, even an abusive one, is rarely easy.

You may feel that you have to stay in the relationship because:

- **You want to protect your children.** You worry that if you leave your spouse will harm your children or prevent you from having access to them. Obtaining custody of children is always challenging for fathers, but even if you are confident that you can do so, you may still feel overwhelmed at the prospect of raising them alone.

- **You feel ashamed.** Many men feel great shame that they've been beaten down by a woman or failed in their role as protector and provider for the family.

- **Your religious beliefs** dictate that you stay or your self-worth is so low that you feel this relationship is all you deserve.

- **There's a lack of resources.** Many men have difficulty being believed by the authorities, or their abuse is minimized because they're male, and can find few resources to help abused men.

- **You're in a same sex relationship but haven't come out** to family or friends, and are afraid your partner will out you.

- **You're in denial.** Just as with female domestic violence victims, denying that there is a problem in your relationship will only prolong the abuse. You may believe that you can help your abuser or she may have promised to change. But change can only happen once your abuser takes full responsibility for her behavior and seeks professional treatment.

You Are Not Alone

If you need immediate assistance, call 911 or your local emergency service.

Abused men can also reach out to the following organizations for help:

- U.S. and Canada: 1-888-7HELPLINE (1-888-743-5754) The Domestic Abuse Helpline
- UK: 01823 334244 ManKind Initiative
- Australia: One in Three Campaign offers a number of crisis hotlines
- Worldwide: SAFE offers crisis hotlines, shelters, and other resources worldwide

If you're a man in an abusive relationship, it's important to know that you're not alone. It happens to men from all cultures and all walks of life. Figures suggest that as many as one in three victims of domestic violence are male. However, men are often reluctant to report abuse by women because they feel embarrassed, or they fear they won't be believed, or worse, that police will assume that since they're male they are the perpetrator of the violence and not the victim.

Asoral Publishing

An abusive wife or partner may hit, kick, bite, punch, spit, throw things, or destroy your possessions. To make up for any difference in strength, she may attack you while you're asleep or otherwise catch you by surprise. She may also use a weapon, such as a gun or knife, or strike you with an object, abuse or threaten your children, or harm your pets. Of course, domestic abuse is not limited to violence. Your spouse or partner may also:

- Verbally abuse you, belittle you, or humiliate you in front of friends, colleagues, or family, or on social media sites

- Be possessive, act jealous, or harass you with accusations of being unfaithful

- Take away your car keys or medications, try to control where you go and who you see

- Try to control how you spend money or deliberately default on joint financial obligations

- Make false allegations about you to your friends, employer, or the police, or find other ways to manipulate and isolate you

- Threaten to leave you and prevent you from seeing your kids if you report the abuse

If you're gay, bisexual, or transgender

You can experience domestic violence if you're in a relationship with someone who:

- Threatens to tell friends, family, colleagues, or community members your sexual orientation or gender identity
- Tells you that authorities won't help a gay, bisexual, or transgender person
- Tells you that leaving the relationship means you're admitting that gay, bisexual, or transgender relationships are deviant
- Justifies abuse by telling you that you're not *really* gay, bisexual, or transgender
- Says that men are naturally violent

Source: Mayo Clinic

Advice and support helplines for abused men

In the U.S. and Canada: Call Domestic Abuse Helpline for Men and Women at 1-888-7HELPLINE (1-888-743-5754).

In the UK: Call ManKind Initiative at 01823 334244 or Men's Advice Line at 0808 801 0327.

In Australia: Visit One in Three Campaign for advice and hotlines.

Worldwide: Visit SAFE for a list of crisis hotlines, shelters, and other resources or International Directory of Domestic Violence Agencies.

Advice and support for gay men who've been abused

In the U.S.: Call Gay Men's Domestic Violence Project at 1-800-832-1901.

In the UK: Call Broken Rainbow UK at 0300 999 5428.

Understanding domestic violence against men

Domestic Violence Against Men: Know the Signs – Learn to identify domestic violence against men and how to break the cycle and get help. (Mayo Clinic)

Safety Planning (PDF) – Tips for safety while in or trying to leave an abusive relationship. (National Domestic Violence Hotline)

Asoral Publishing

Against Men

According to a British:

- More married men suffer abuse from their spouse than married women

- These days, women move more in men's worlds

- They earn and compete with as much aggression as their male colleagues

- Women are also fast catching up with men in the alcohol stakes

Source: dailymail.co.uk

Safety

Safety Plan

Create a safety plan

Leaving an abuser can be dangerous. Consider taking these precautions:

- Call a domestic violence hotline for advice. Make the call at a safe time — when the abuser isn't around — or from a friend's house or other safe location.

- Pack an emergency bag that includes items you'll need when you leave, such as extra clothes and keys. Leave the bag in a safe place. Keep important personal papers, money and prescription medications handy so that you can take them with you on short notice.

- Know exactly where you'll go and how you'll get there.

Protect your communication and location

An abuser can use technology to monitor your telephone and online communication and to track your physical location. If you're concerned for your safety, seek help. To maintain your privacy:

Safety

- **Use phones cautiously.** Your abuser might intercept calls and listen to your conversations. He or she might use caller ID, check your cellphone or search your phone billing records to see your complete call and texting history.

- **Use your home computer cautiously.** Your abuser might use spyware to monitor your emails and the websites you visit. Consider using a computer at work, at the library or at a friend's house to seek help.

- **Remove GPS devices from your vehicle.** Your abuser might use a GPS device to pinpoint your location.

- **Frequently change your email password.** Choose a password that would be impossible for your abuser to guess.

- **Clear your viewing history.** Follow your browser's instructions to clear any record of websites or graphics you've viewed.

Safety

Where to seek help

In an emergency, call 911 — or your local emergency number or law enforcement agency. The following resources also can help:

- **Someone you trust.** Turn to a friend, relative, neighbor, co-worker or religious or spiritual adviser for support.

- **National Domestic Violence Hotline: 800-799-SAFE or 800-799-7233.** The hotline provides crisis intervention and referrals to resources.

- **Your health care provider.** Doctors and nurses will treat injuries and can refer you to other local resources.

- **A counseling or mental health center.** Counseling and support groups for people in abusive relationships are available in most communities.

- **A local court.** Your district court can help you obtain a restraining order that legally mandates the abuser to stay away from you or face arrest. Local advocates may be available to help guide you through the process.

Domestic violence against men can have devastating effects. Although you may not be able to stop your partner's abusive behavior, you can seek help. Remember, no one deserves to be abused.

Asoral Publishing

Safety

SAFETY AT HOME

Develop a safety plan and discuss it with your children. Review the plan as often as possible. Change the locks and install devices to secure your windows. Make sure your children's school, day-care center, or camp knows who is authorized to pick up your children. Tell your neighbors and landlord that your abuser no longer lives there and ask them to call the police if they see him or her near your home. Before you resume a potentially abusive relationship, discuss alternatives with someone you trust.

SAFETY IN PUBLIC OR AT WORK

If you have an order of protection, keep it with you at all times. Inform building security and coworkers you trust of your situation. If possible, provide a photograph of your abuser to building security. Vary your routes to and from work and arrange for someone to escort you to your car, bus, or train. Plan what to do in various situations if the abuser confronts you.

SAFETY DURING VOLATILE DOMESTIC VIOLENCE INCIDENT

If an argument seems unavoidable, move to a room or area with easy access to an exit - not a bathroom, kitchen, or anywhere near weapons. Identify which door, window, stairwell or elevator offers the quickest way out of the home - and practice your route. Have a bag packed and ready. Keep it in an undisclosed but

Safety

accessible place where you can retrieve it quickly. Find neighbors you can tell about the violence and ask that they call the police if they hear a disturbance. Devise a code word to use with your children, family, and friends when you need the police. Decide where you will go if you have to leave, even if you do not think it will come to that. Use your instincts and judgment. Consider giving the abuser what he or she wants to defuse a dangerous situation. You have a right to protect yourself when you are in danger. You do not deserve to be battered or threatened.

Safety

PERSONALIZED SAFETY PLAN (example)

The following steps represent my plan for increasing my safety and preparing in advance for the possibility for further violence. Although I do not have control over my partner's violence, I do have a choice about how to respond to him/her and how to best get myself and my children to safety.

Step 1: SAFETY DURING A VIOLENT INCIDENT. Women cannot always avoid violent incidents. In order to increase safety, battered women may use a variety of strategies.

I can use some or all of the following strategies:

A. If I decide to leave, I will _____.
(Practice how to get out safely. What doors, windows, elevators, stairwells or fire escapes would you use?)

B. I can keep my purse and car keys ready and put them _____ _____ (place) in order to leave quickly.

C. I can tell _____ about the violence and request they call the police if they hear suspicious noises coming from my house.

D. I can teach my children how to use the telephone to contact the police and the fire department.

Safety

E. I will use _____ as my code for my children or my friends so they can call for help.

F. If I have to leave my home, I will go _____ _____ (Decide this even if you don't think there will be a next time). If I cannot go to the location above, then I can go to _____ _____or_____ _____.

G. I can also teach some of these strategies to some/all of my children.

H. When I expect we are going to have an argument, I will try to move to a space that is lowest risk, such as _____ _____. (Try to avoid arguments in the bathroom, garage, kitchen, near weapons or in rooms without access to an outside door).

I. I will use my judgment and intuition. If the situation is very serious, I can give my partner what he/she wants to calm him/her down. I have to protect myself until I/we are out of danger.

Step 2: SAFETY WHEN PREPARING TO LEAVE. Battered women frequently leave the residence they share with the battering partner. Leaving must be

Safety

done with a careful plan in order to increase safety. Batterers often strike back when they believe that a battered woman is leaving the relationship.

I can use some or all the following safety strategies:

A. I will leave money and an extra set of keys with_____ so that I can leave quickly.

B. I will keep copies of important papers and documents or an extra set of keys at
_____.

C. I will open a savings account by _____, to increase my independence.

D. Other things I can do to increase my independence include:

E. The domestic violence program's hot line telephone number is _____ and I can seek shelter by calling this hot line.

F. I can keep change for phone calls on me at all times. I understand that if I use my telephone credit card, the following month the telephone bill will tell my batterer those numbers that I called after I left. To keep my telephone communications confidential, I must either use coins or I might get a friend to permit me to use their telephone credit card for a limited time when I first leave.

Safety

G. I will check with
_____ and
_____ to see who would be able to let me stay with them or lend me some money in an emergency.

H. I can leave extra clothes with_____.

I. I will sit down and review my safety plan every _____ in order to plan the safest way to leave the residence.

_____

_ (domestic violence advocate or friend) has agreed to help me review this plan.

J. I will rehearse my escape plan and, as appropriate, practice it with my children.

Step 3: SAFETY IN MY OWN RESIDENCE. There are many things that a woman can do to increase her safety in her own residence. It may be impossible to do everything at once, but safety measures can be added step by step.

Safety measures I can use include:

A. I can change the locks on my doors and windows as soon as possible.

B. I can replace wooden doors with steel/metal doors.

Safety

C. I can install security systems including additional locks, window bars, poles to wedge against doors, an electronic system, etc.

D. I can purchase rope ladders to be used for escape from second floor windows.

E. I can install smoke detectors and purchase fire extinguishers for each floor in my house/apartment.

F. I can install an outside lighting system that lights up when a person is coming close to my house.

G. I will teach my children how to use the telephone to make a collect call to me and to _____ (friend/minister/other) in the event that my partner takes the children.

H. I will tell people who take care of my children which people have permission to pick up my children and that my partner is not permitted to do so. The people I will inform about pick-up permission include:

_____
(school),

_____ (day care staff),

_____
(babysitter),

_____ (Sunday School

Safety

teacher),

_____

(teacher),

_____ (and),

_____

(others),

I. I can inform
_____, and
_____ (neighbors),
_____ (pastor),
and,_____ (friend) that my partner no longer resides with me and they should call the police if he is observed near my residence.

I can find out my risks with Rate Your Risk Tests.

Step 4: SAFETY WITH AN ORDER OF PROTECTION. Many battered women obey protection orders, but one can never be sure which violent partner will obey and which will violate protection orders. I recognize that I may need to ask the police and the court to enforce my protection order.

The following are some steps that I can take to help the enforcement of my protection order:

A. I will keep my protection order_____

Safety

(location) (Always keep it on or near your person. If you change purses, that's the first thing that should go in).

B. I will give my protection order to police departments in the communities where I usually visit family or friends, and in the community where I live.

C. The Clark County Sheriff is the county registry of protection orders that all police departments can call to confirm a protection order. I can check to make sure that my order is in registry. The telephone number for the county registry of protection order is

_____.

D. For further safety, if I often visit other counties in Indiana, I might file my protection order with the court in those counties.

E. I can call the local domestic violence program if I have questions or if I have some problem with my protection order.

F. I will inform my employer, my minister, my closest friend, my relatives, and

_____

_____and

_____tha t I have a protection order in effect.

G. If my partner destroys my protection order, I can get another copy from the Clark County Courthouse by going to the Circuit Court Clerk's Office, or by

Safety

contacting the Domestic Violence Unit of the Clark County Prosecuting Attorney.

H. If my partner violates the protection order, I can call the police and report a violation, contact my attorney, call my advocate, and/or advise the court of the violation.

I. If the police do no help, I can contact my advocate or attorney and will file a complaint with the chief of the police department.

J. I can also file a private criminal compliant with the Prosecuting Attorney in the jurisdiction where the violation occurred. I can request that charges be filed against my battering partner for violation of the Protective Order and all the crimes that he commits in violating the order. I can call the domestic violence advocate for help.

Step 5: SAFETY ON THE JOB AND IN PUBLIC. Each battered woman must decide if and when she will tell others that her partner has battered her and that she may be at continued risk. Friends, family and co-workers can help to protect women. Each woman should consider carefully which people to invite to help secure her safety.

I might do any or all of the following:

A. I can inform my boss, the security supervisor and_____ at work of my situation.

Safety

B. I can ask _____ to help screen my telephone calls at work.

C. When leaving work, I can _____.

D. When driving home if problems occur, I can _____.

E. If I use public transit, I can _____.

F. I will go to different grocery stores and shopping malls to conduct my business and shop at hours that are different than those when residing with my battered partner.

G. I can use a different bank and take care of my banking at hours different from those I used when residing with my battered partner.

H. I can also_____ _____.

Step 6: SAFETY AND DRUG OR ALCOHOL USE. Most people in this culture use alcohol. Many use mood-altering drugs. Much of this use is legal and some is not. The legal outcomes of using illegal drugs can be very hard on a battered woman, may hurt her relationship with her children and put her at a disadvantage in other legal actions with her battering partner. Therefore, women should carefully consider the

Safety

potential cost of the use of illegal drugs. But beyond this, the use of any alcohol or other drug can reduce a woman's awareness and ability to act quickly to protect herself from her battering partner. Furthermore, the use of alcohol or other drugs by the batterer may give him/her an excuse to use violence. Therefore, in the context of drug or alcohol use, a woman needs to make specific safety plans.

If drug or alcohol use has occurred in my relationship with the battering partner, I can enhance my safety by some or all of the following:

A. If I am going to use, I can do so in a safe place and with people who understand the risk of violence and are committed to my safety.

B. I can also_____.

C. If my partner is using, I can_____.

D. I might also_____.

E. To safeguard my children, I might _____and _____ _.

Step 7: SAFETY AND MY EMOTIONAL HEALTH. The experience of being battered and

Safety

verbally degraded by partners is usually exhausting and emotionally draining. The process of building a new life for myself takes much courage and incredible energy.

To conserve my emotional energy and resources and to avoid hard emotional times, I can do some of the following:

A. If I feel down and ready to return to a potentially abusive situation, I can _____.

B. When I have to communicate with my partner in person or by telephone, I can _____.

C. I can try to use "I can . . . " statements with myself and to be assertive with others.

D. I can tell myself - "_____
_____" whenever I feel others are trying to control or abuse me.

E. I can read _____ to help me feel stronger.

F. I can call _____, _____ and _____ as other resources to be of support of me.

Safety

G. Other things I can do to help me feel stronger are_____ _____,
and_____.

H. I can attend workshops and support groups at the domestic violence program or

_____
_____, or _____to gain support and strengthen my relationships with other people.

Step 8: Items to take when leaving. When women leave partners, it is important to take certain items with them. Beyond this, women sometimes give an extra copy of papers and an extra set of clothing to a friend just in case they have to leave quickly.

Money : Even if I have never worked, I may be entitled to the funds in the checking and savings accounts. If I don't take any money from the accounts, he can legally take all money and/or close the account and I may not get my share until the court rules on it if ever.

Items with asterisks on the following list are the most important to take. If there is time, the other items might be taken, or stored outside the home. These items might be placed in one location, so that if we have to leave in a hurry, I can grab them quickly.

When I leave, I should have:

* Identification for myself
*Children's birth certificate
*My birth certificate

Safety

*Social security cards
*School and vaccination records
*Money
*Checkbook, ATM (Automatic Tellers Machine) card, Credit cards
*Keys - house/car/office
*Driver's license and registration
*Medication
Welfare identification, work permits, Green Card, Passport, divorce papers
Medical records - for all family members
Lease/rental agreement, house deed, mortgage payment book
Bank books, Insurance papers
Small saleable objects
Address book, pictures, jewelry
Children's favorite toys and/or blankets
Items of special sentimental value

Telephone numbers I need to know:

Emergency: 911
Indiana State Police (812) 246-5424
Clark County Police (812) 283-4471
Clark County Sheriff (812) 283-4471
Jeffersonville Police (812) 283-6633
Clarksville Police (812) 288-7151
Sellersburg Police (812) 246-4491
Charlestown Police (812) 256-6345
Utica Town Marshal (812) 283-4471
Borden Town Marshal (812) 967-5464

Safety

Clark County Prosecuting Attorney
Domestic Violence Unit - (812) 285-6264

Center for Women and Families
(812) 944-6743 or (502) 581-7222

National Domestic Violence Hotline
1-800-799-SAFE (24 hour / toll-free)

Indiana Coalition Against Domestic Violence, Inc.
1-800-332-7385

County Registry of Protection Orders
Clark County Sheriff (812) 283-4471

Work number_____

Supervisor's home number_____

Minister_____

Other_____

I will keep this document in a safe place and out of the reach of my potential attacker.

Review date:_____

Asoral Publishing

Safety

IF YOU NEED HELP IN FILLING OUT THIS PLAN YOU MAY ASK POLICE DETECTIVES, COUNSELORS, SHELTER WORKERS, THE CENTER FOR WOMEN AND FAMILIES, THE DOMESTIC VIOLENCE UNIT OF THE CLARK COUNTY PROSECUTING ATTORNEY, OR A CLOSE AND TRUSTED FRIEND.

Source: clarkcountyprosecutor.org

Safety

Safety Plan for Stalking

WHAT IS STALKING?

Stalking is one person's obsessive behavior directed toward another person, behavior that causes the victim to fear for his/her safety. The stalker usually starts with annoying, obscene, or threatening phone calls or written communications within a short time after separation or divorce.

The stalker may move from harassing communication to following the victim, and staking out workplaces and home. There may be acts of violence targeted at the victim's property, pets, and the victim herself/himself. But keep in mind that human behavior cannot be accurately predicted, so it is impossible to gauge when and if a stalker will become violent. However, remember that stalking is rooted in obsessive behavior, which in and of itself is dangerous.

WHAT SHOULD A STALKING VICTIM DO?

1) Do your best to safely avoid all contact with the stalker.

2) Inform family, friends, and co-workers of what is going on regarding the stalking behavior.

3) Report the stalking to the police and follow their advice.

4) Keep a journal or log of all stalking incidents.

Safety

5) Keep all letters, packages, e-mails messages, facsimiles, and taped telephone messages received from the stalker.

WORKING WITH LAW ENFORCEMENT

The police or sheriff's department will actively investigate matters concerning _____

_____
_____ (depends on state statute).

Although it is their intention to provide you with a professional investigative service, please be advised that the police or sheriff's department cannot guarantee that your situation will be resolved, nor can they guarantee your safety.

Unfortunately, there is no way to predict human behavior. Suspects may be mentally disordered or may be substance abusers. A lethality assessment is always situational, based upon an evolving and changing set of factors.

Based upon available information, the police or sheriff's department can provide you with security recommendations, which will help you make your own decisions on how to best secure your safety.

Should you feel that additional security measures are required, such as a domestic violence shelter, you are certainly entitled to avail yourself of these measures.

Safety

Your cooperation by working within the criminal justice system is necessary for the proper investigation of this matter and is greatly appreciated. Please do not hesitate to contact the police or sheriff's department should any questions or concerns arise.

RESIDENTIAL SECURITY

~ All adults in the house should be trained in the use of any fi rearm kept for protection. The firearm should be stored safely and away from children.

~ Household staff/employees should have a thorough background check before employment. Institute and strictly enforce a policy that prohibits the staff from discussing family matters.

~ Be aware of any unusual packages, boxes, or devices found on the premises. Do not investigate strange objects; call the police or sheriff's department immediately.

~ Install smoke detectors and maintain fi re extinguishers on all levels of the residence.

~ Tape emergency contact numbers on each phone in the residence.

~ When leaving the residence for a period of time, have lights, television, and radio set on a timer.

~ Have a thorough safety plan that incorporates an emergency evacuation plan.

Asoral Publishing

Safety

~ Purchase a dog; dogs are an inexpensive alarm system. Hint: Dogs purchased by or familiar with

The stalker provides no protection!

~ Know the daily schedule/whereabouts of all family members.

~ Accompany children to school or bus stops.

~ Vary daily routines, such as your route to work, etc.

~ Require identification from all service people and salespeople before permitting them to enter the residence.

~ Try to park in a secured area such as a garage when possible. Inform a trusted neighbor of the situation and provide her or him with a vehicle and suspect description.

SECURITY RECOMMENDATIONS

~ Be alert at all times for suspicious persons.

~ Positively identify persons before opening the door -- install wide-angle viewers in primary doors.

~ Install a porch light at a height that discourages removal.

Safety

~ Install dead-bolt locks on all outside doors. If keys are missing, replace all locks. You may want to replace all the locks regardless, assuming the stalker may have made a copy of the key(s).

~ Keep the garage door locked at all times. Use an electric garage-door opener.

~ Install floodlights around your residence that are on a timer or that have motion activation.

~ Trim shrubbery, especially away from doors and windows.

~ Keep your fuse box locked. Have flashlights, candles, and lanterns throughout the house.

~ Install a loud exterior alarm that can be activated from several places within the residence.

~ Maintain an unlisted phone number.

~ Any written, e-mailed, or telephone threats should be treated as legitimate and the police or sheriff's department should be notifi ed.

~ Inform trusted neighbors of any anticipated vacation and/or business trips, and arrange for someone to pick up the mail, newspapers, etc.

~ If residing in an apartment complex, provide the manager and security guard with a picture of the suspect.

Safety

~ If you are considering purchasing a gun for your protection, weigh your decision based on these cautions:

1. The offender may use it against you.

2. Most people hesitate to shoot an intruder.

3. There is potential for accidental injury, especially if you have children in the house.

(You should consider taking handgun lessons to learn proper weapon handling, safety, and familiarity, as well as the legal aspects of deadly force. Some states may require this in order to purchase the handgun.)

WORKPLACE SECURITY

~ If you have a security guard or agency, inform them of the situation and provide them with a photograph and a description of the suspect.

~ Have a secretary or co-worker screen calls.

~ Have a secretary or security screen all incoming mail and packages.

~ Be aware of people following you to and from work.

~ Do not accept any packages unless you personally ordered them.

~ Central reception should handle all visitors and packages.

Safety

~ Office staff should be aware of the situation so they are alert to suspicious people, parcels, or packages.

~ Establish lock-and-key control: Change locks if the keys of terminated employees are unaccounted for.

~ Park in a secured area if possible.

~ Have your name removed from your reserved parking spot, if applicable.

PERSONAL SECURITY

~ Obtain a mailbox address and file a change of address with the Post Office.

~ Send a note to friends, businesses, etc., giving them your new address and requesting that they remove your old address from their files.

~ All current creditors should be given the new address and remove the old from their system.

~ Obtain a new driver's license and file a change of address with the motor vehicle department,

~ Remove your home address from personal checks and business cards.

~ Destroy discarded mail.

Safety

~ Telephone lines can be installed in a location other than your residence and call forwarded to your home.

~ Place residential agreements in a trusted friend's or relative's name.

~ Your name should not appear on service or delivery orders to the residence.

~ Record activities such as vandalism or property damage.

~ Keep a log of the stalker's activities.

~ Leaving a violent relationship is oftentimes dangerous and a safety plan is necessary.

~ Discuss with the police or sheriff's department whether you qualify for a protection order.

(Protection orders, when properly enforced, enhance your safety and aid law enforcement in holding the offender accountable for his behavior.)

WHAT IS A PROTECTION ORDER? (Consult state statute for specifics.)

~ Contact a shelter or district attorney for details on protection orders, the application process, and related details.

~ A protection order is a paper signed by a judge to protect a victim from certain people who have battered or threatened them. In some states, protection orders are

Safety

available against stalkers as well. The protection order may be able to be obtained without having a lawyer.

~ Persons abused by family or household members are eligible.

~ All courts can issue orders of protection.

~ Typical process of obtaining the order:

- Victim files petition with clerk of the court

- Clerk provides forms and assistance

- Emergency protection order is issued by judge at ex-parte hearing

- Full hearing is held within 30 days; if continuance is necessary, the emergency protection order is extended for 30 days

- Full order is issued after the hearing, is in place for one year, and can be renewed

~ Possible terms of the order:

- Enjoin from abuse, harassment, direct, or indirect contact

- Stay away orders

- Award possession of the residence

- Temporary child custody and visitation arrangements

Safety

- Payment of shelter costs

- Awarding custody of property

- Counseling

~ The respondent (suspect) must be served before a full hearing can be held. Service is done by the sheriff or another law enforcement officer.

~ Violation of the protection order is contempt of court, a Class B misdemeanor (depending on the state statute). Subsequent violations may induce felony charges.

NOTE: Please be aware that you are not necessarily safe because you have fi led for a protective order. The suspect may choose to violate the order like s/he has the criminal statutes. Remain safety conscious.

RESOURCE NUMBERS

Emergency numbers:

Local police/911

_____

_____

State police

_____

_____

Asoral Publishing

Safety

Victim/witness services
_____

_____

Emergency shelter:

YWCA shelter
_____

_____

Local domestic violence shelter
_____

_____

Legal help:

Victim/witness services
_____

_____

Local domestic violence shelter
_____

_____

Lawyer referral services
_____

_____

Prosecutor's office
_____

_____

Safety

Court clerk (protection order)

_____
_____

National Domestic Violence Hotline: 1-800-799-SAFE (7233) www.ndvh.org

1-800-787-3224 (TTY)

National Stalking Resource Center: 1-800-FYI-CALL (394-2255) www.ncvc.org/src

(Monday to Friday, 8:30 a.m. - 8:30 p.m. EST)

Safety

College Student Safety Plan

WHY DO I NEED A SAFETY PLAN?

Everyone deserves a relationship that is healthy, safe and supportive. If you are in a relationship that is hurting you, it is important for you to know that the abuse is not your fault. It is also important for you to start thinking of ways to keep yourself safe from the abuse, whether you decide to end the relationship or not. While you can't control your partner's abusive behavior, you can take action to keep yourself as safe as possible.

WHAT IS A SAFETY PLAN?

A safety plan is a practical guide that helps lower your risk of being hurt by your abuser. It includes information specific to you and your life that will help keep you safe.

A good safety plan helps you think through lifestyle changes that will help keep you as safe as possible on campus, in the dorms and other places that you go on a daily basis.

HOW DO I MAKE A SAFETY PLAN?

Take some time for yourself to go through each section of this safety plan. You can complete the workbook on your own, or you can work through it with someone else that you trust.

Keep in Mind:

Safety

· In order for this safety plan to work for you, you'll need to fill in personalized answers, so you can use the information when you most need it.

· Once you complete your safety plan, be sure to keep it in an

accessible but secure location. You might also consider giving a copy of your safety plan to someone that you trust.

· Getting support from someone who has experience working with college students in abusive relationships can be very useful.

Staying Safe on Campus:
The safest way for me to get to class is:
_____
_____

These are places on campus where I often run into my abuser:
_____,_____
__and _____. I will try and avoid those places as much as possible or try to go when s/he won't be there.
There may be places on campus where it is impossible to avoid my abuser. If I need to go to one of those places I can make sure a friend can go with me. I will ask_____,
_____and/or_____
_____.

Safety

If I feel threatened or unsafe when I am on campus, I can go to these public areas where I feel safe (dining hall, quad, etc.):

_____
_____and/or_____

I could talk to the following people if I need to rearrange my schedule or transfer dorms in order to avoid my abuser; or if I need help staying safe on campus:
Campus Police
Resident Advisor
Professors:_____

Dorm Security_____
Dean of Students_____
Sexual Assault Center_____
Women's Center_____
LGBTQ Center_____
Counselor_____
Other:_____

Staying Safe in the Dorms

I can tell these people (hall mates, roommates or RA's) about what is going on in my relationship:
_____,

Safety

_____and_____
_____.

There will be times when my roommate is gone. If I feel unsafe during those times, I can have people stay with me. I will ask:

_____
_____.

The safest way for me to leave the dorms in an emergency is:

_____
_____.

If I have to leave the dorms in an emergency, I should try to go to a place that is public, safe and unknown by my abuser. I could go here:

_____
and/or
here:_____
_____.

I will use a code word so I can alert my family, friends, roommates and/or hall mates to call for help without my abuser knowing about it. My code word is:

_____
_____.

Safety

If I live with or near my abuser, I will have a bag ready with these important items in case I need to leave quickly (check all that ap-ply):
Cell phone & charger
Spare money
Keys
Driver's license or other form of ID
Copy of Restraining Order
Birth certificate,
Social Security card,
immigration papers and other important documents
Change of clothes
Medications
Special photos or other valuable items
If I have children—anything they may need (important papers, formula, diapers)

Staying Safe Emotionally:
My abuser often makes me feel bad by saying this:
_____
_____
_____
_____.

When he/she does this, I will think of these reasons why I know my abuser is wrong:
_____
_____,
_____
_ and
_____
_____.

Safety

I will do things I enjoy, like: _____ _____, _____ _ and _____ _____.
I will join clubs or organizations that interest me, like: _____ or _____.

If I feel confused, depressed or scared, I can call the following friends or family members:
Name:_____
Phone #: _____
Name:_____
Phone #: _____
Name:_____
Phone #: _____
Name:_____
Phone #: _____

Safety

Getting Help in Your Community:
For emergencies: 911
National Dating Abuse Helpline: 1-866-331-9474

Campus police station:
Phone #: _____
Location:
_____

Campus Health Center:
_____
Phone #:
_____
Location: _____
Campus Women's or LGBTQ Center:
_____
Phone #: _____
Location:
_____

Local Free Legal Assistance:
_____
Phone #:
_____
Address:
_____

During an emergency, I can call the following friends, family members or residential life staff at any time of day or night:
Name:_____

Safety

Phone #: _____
Name:_____
Phone #: _____
Name:_____
Phone #: _____
Name:_____
Phone #: _____

Asoral Publishing

Safety

Tips

These are things I can do to help keep myself safe everyday:

1. I will carry my cell phone and important telephone numbers with me at all times.

2. I will keep in touch with someone I trust about where I am or what I am doing.

3. I will stay out of isolated places and try to never walk around alone.

4. If possible, I will alert dorm or campus security about what is happening in my relationship so that my abuser is not allowed in my building.

5. I will avoid places where my abuser or his/her friends and family are likely to be.

6. I will keep the doors and windows locked where I live, especially if I am alone.

7. I will avoid speaking to my abuser. If it is unavoidable, I will make sure there are people around in case the situation becomes dangerous.

8. I will call 911 if I feel my safety is at risk.

Safety

9. I can look into getting a protective order so that I'll have legal support in keeping my abuser away.

10. I can see if there are any self-defense classes available at my college or university.

11. I will remember that the abuse is not my fault and that I deserve a safe and healthy relationship.

These are things I can do to help keep myself safe in my social life:

1. I will ask my friends to keep their cell phones with them while they are with me in case we get separated and I need help.

2. If possible, I will go to different malls, bars, banks, parties, grocery stores, movie theaters, dining halls, etc. than the ones my abuser goes to or knows about.

3. I will avoid going out alone, especially at night.

4. No matter where I go, I will be aware of how to leave safely in case of an emergency.

5. I will leave if I feel uncomfortable in a situation, no matter what my friends are doing.

Safety

6. If I plan on drinking, I will be sure to have a sober driver who is *not* my abuser.

7. I will spend time with people who make me feel safe, supported and good about myself.

These are things I can do to stay safe online and with my cell phone:

1. I will not say or do anything online that I wouldn't in person.

2. I will set all my online profiles to be as private as they can be.

3. I will save and keep track of any abusive, threatening or harassing comments, posts, or texts.

4. I will never give my password to anyone.

5. If the abuse and harassment does not stop, I will change my usernames, email addresses, and/or cell phone number.

6. I will not answer calls from unknown, blocked or private numbers.

Asoral Publishing

Safety

7. I can see if my phone company can block my abuser's phone number from calling my phone.

8. I will not communicate with my abuser using any type of technology if unnecessary, since any form of communication can be recorded and possibly used against me in the future.

Safety Planning for persons with Disabilities

PLANNING FOR AN EXPLOSIVE INCIDENT

♦ **Set-up alternative personal assistance if needed.** Call ahead and talk with a caseworker, independent living center, or disability organization to identify emergency personal attendant (PA)/caregivers if you foresee the need to leave or have an abusive PA/caregiver removed. Contact a trustworthy friend or family member to arrange a transition period PA/caregiver.

♦ **Practice how to get out of your home safely if possible.** Visualize your escape route and means of escaping. Identify the best doors, elevator, or stairwell. If you are unable to exit, try to position yourself where shouting may attract attention (keep windows partially open, or move near to a wall attached to another apartment or building).

Safety

♦ **Have ready** spare medication, medical supplies and adaptive equipment, money, change or a telephone card, extra set of keys, and clothes for you and your children/grandchildren. Keep these items in one place so they can be obtained if you have to leave quickly. Seek the help of a safe person if you need assistance.

Plan ahead for where you will go, if you have to leave. You or a safe individual/agency can contact a domestic violence shelter to discuss whether their facility is accessible. Ask the following: Are PA/caregiver services available? Can PA/caregiver accompany person? Are there rules that require someone seeking shelter to be dropped off at alternate location and if there is an exception for a person with a disability? If the shelter it is not accessible, or you do not wish to use a shelter, locate an alternative safe haven option.

♦ **Ask a neighbor, or someone who has regular contact to call the police** if they hear a disturbance or have not seen you for a period of time. Also, have other individuals you regularly visit (doctor, PA/caregiver, caseworker) contact police or adult protective services if you miss appointments (if this will not place you in further danger). Consider other individuals such as delivery people, postal workers and van

Safety

drivers who can also contact police if behavior or routine changes.

♦ **Devise a code word or signal** to use with your children, grandchildren, PA/caregiver, friends, doctor, and others to communicate you need the police.

Safety

SAFETY DURING AN EXPLOSIVE INCIDENT

◦ **Plan out actions and safety precautions during a non-explosive period.**

◦ If you can see an argument coming, (often you cannot), **try to go to a room or area that has an accessible exit.** Do not go to a bathroom (near hard surfaces), a kitchen (knives) or any room with weapons. If you have mobility limitations, see if you can have your PA/caregiver move you to a safer room. If your PA/caregiver is your abuser, make an excuse for the move unless it would only further escalate the situation.

◦ Try to **stay in a room with a telephone** so you can call 911, the police, a friend or a neighbor. Keep a cordless or cellular telephone with you if possible. You may be able to tuck it by your side, in your wheelchair, walker or scooter. Turn the ringer off so your abuser does not become aware of the telephone. Program 911 and other safety numbers into the speed dial for easier use. If you have difficulty with verbal communication, use a cordless telephone where a call to 911 can be traced and assistance will normally be sent regardless of verbal communication. Consider a medical alert device, which can be worn at all times without suspicion, and used to call for help.

Safety

- If you need personal assistance with tasks and your PA/caregiver is your abuser, try to **have assistance done early in the day** when, you are as mobile and alert as possible in case of an emergency. Make sure to keep mobility and other necessary aids nearby. If the PA/caregiver is your abuser, try not to have them perform personal tasks (like bathing, toileting, dressing, transferring, etc.) at times when the PA/caregiver is agitated or has been drinking. You are at greater risk of physical injury during those times.

- If weapons are in the home, **inform law enforcement, adult protective services or your caseworker.**

- **Use your instinct and judgment.** If a situation is very dangerous and you are unable to escape or have your abuser removed, consider any action that might calm things down. Try to give yourself time to assess what action you can take or assistance you can get to keep safe.

- Always remember – **YOU DO NOT DESERVE TO BE THREATENED OR HIT!**

Safety

SAFETY WHEN PREPARING TO LEAVE

☐ **Open a saving account** in your own name to establish or increase your independence. If you receive Social Security (SSI/SSDI) benefit checks, have them directly deposited in that account. It can take a couple months for the direct deposit change, so plan ahead if possible. Be prepared to intercept confirmation letter that Social Security will send.

☐ **Open a post office box** where you can receive mail unknown to your abuse. Find a trusted friend, family member, PA/caregiver, or case manager that can assist in getting items from the post office box if needed.

☐ **If you have a payee** for your SSI/SSDI benefits and the payee is your abuser, contact the Social Security Administration to change your payee. You may be able to get assistance through a caseworker, domestic violence shelter, disabilities organization or adult protective services. Again, caution is important because loss of financial control may be perceived as threatening to the abuser and the violence may escalate.

☐ **Leave or have someone assist you in leaving** money, extra keys, copies of important documents (birth certificate, marriage license, Social Security award letter, etc.), and extra

Safety

clothes with someone you trust so you can leave quickly.

- **Bring any medications**, prescriptions, glasses, hearing aids, or other assistive devices you need. When appropriate, plan how a service animal can accompany you. Keep all these items together in one place so they are easily available.

- **Determine who** you can stay with temporarily, and who can lend you money. Contact your caseworker, independent living center and/or, county/tribal aging unit to identify emergency or other financial benefits you may be entitled to after leaving your abuser.

- See "Planning for an Explosive Incident" (page 2) if you need personal assistance. Try to build **a network of friends, family members, and faith community members** who can provide assistance during your transition. You must plan ahead for PA/caregiver services as needed so they are available at the time of leaving. The more prepared the new PA/caregiver is for the emergency situation, the more likely they will be able to provide good and safe care.

Keep the domestic abuse program number close at hand, written down where abuser will not find it or give to a safe individual to contact for you. Keep some change or a telephone calling card with you at all times for emergency

Safety

telephone calls. Consider programming the domestic violence shelter number into a cellular telephone. Find out if the shelter is physically accessible for you, and if not, search for other safe emergency housing. Remember to ask about whether PA/caregiver service is available at the shelter or if your PA/caregiver will be able to come to the shelter to assist you. For those with hearing impairments, contact or have someone safe contact the shelter, prior to an emergency, to check if the shelter has a TTY or other safe means of communication.

- **Plan for transportation to leave an abusive situation or seek support.** Make sure your vehicle and any adaptations are in working order. Keep the gas tank at least half full so you always have enough gas if you need to leave in a hurry. Most transportation services require 24-hour notice so you will have to plan your leaving in advance. Use care to keep your abuser from learning your plans. If you use special transportation services, give the transit company the name of a place you regularly go but not the address of where you really want to go, so your abuser will not get suspicious. If you are not currently using special transportation services and are eligible, consider applying.

- **Review your safety plan** as often as possible in order to plan the safest way to leave. Keep safe friends, family and others who can assist you in leaving informed.

REMEMBER – LEAVING CAN BE THE MOST DANGEROUS TIME.

SAFETY IN YOUR HOME
(if your abuser does not live with you)

▪ **Have the locks changed** on your doors as soon as possible. Buy additional locks, safety devices, and/or security system to secure your windows and doors (keep closed and locked at all times even when expecting visitors). Consider installing or increasing outside lighting.
A locksmith or your landlord can help install extra security devices. You may be able to receive financial assistance through victim assistance programs.

▪ If you have young children, grandchildren, or other dependents living with you, **devise a safety plan** for when you are not with them. Inform their school, day care, etc., about who has permission to pick them up and who does not.

▪ **Inform neighbors, landlord, and other individuals you regularly see** (postal workers, delivery people, and van drivers) that your abuser no longer lives with you. Ask them to call the police if they see your abuser near you, your home or your work.

Safety

☐ Find friends, family members, faith community members, PA/caregivers, postal workers, delivery people, van drivers or others that can **check on you regularly.**

☐ **Change your telephone number and e-mail address** and have the new number unlisted and unpublished. You may be able to get financial assistance through victim assistance.

☐ **Screen telephones calls** by either an answering machine, caller identification, or assistance of another. Keep a record of harassing or threatening telephone calls and e-mail messages by your abuser.

☐ **Inform the police** of the domestic violence situation and your special needs if your abuser attempts to harass or assault you. Have a written note or other means of communicating (number to call) that will let police know about history and extent of abuse if verbal communication is difficult or not possible.

☐ You, your friends, neighbors and others who are regularly in your neighborhood can **watch for stalking behavior from your abuser.** Keep a log of when, where and who saw your abuser near you.

Safety

SAFETY WITH A RESTRAINING ORDER

▪ **For information on obtaining a protection/restraining order** contact or have someone contact a local domestic violence program/shelter or your local clerk of court.

▪ If you obtain a protection/restraining order ask the court to order your **abuser to stay at least 500 feet away from you** at all times.

▪ **Keep your protection/restraining order with you at all times.** When you change your purse, wallet, wheelchair or scooter pack, this should be the first thing you place in it. If you lose or damage your protection/restraining order, you should get another authenticated copy for a small fee from the county or tribal clerk of court office. Keep extra copies of your protection/restraining order where you can find them in case your abuser takes your copy.

▪ If you have a **valid protection/restraining order issued by another state or tribe,** it is enforceable where you now live. **The Full Faith and Credit federal and state law requires all states and Indian tribes to enforce "valid" protection/restraining orders issued by another state or Indian tribe.** This means a protection/restraining order issued in one jurisdiction must be enforced by all other jurisdictions. Even if a person would not be

Safety

eligible for a protection/restraining order in the new state or Indian land, the new state or tribe must still enforce the valid protection/restraining order from another state or Indian land as it is originally written.

A person with an out-of-state or other Indian tribal protection/restraining order should contact a domestic violence agency in their current state or Indian tribe to find out if there are any special procedures for interstate enforcement. Police officers should enforce out-of-state or other Indian tribe protection/restraining orders if they contain both parties' names and have not yet expired. Police officers are often concerned about liability for false arrest in enforcing out-of-state or other Indian tribe protection/restraining orders without contacting the court. Yet, officers should also be aware that they may face liability for failure to arrest.

- **Call or have someone contact the police** if your abuser violates the conditions of the restraining order. Document with the police every violation.

- **Think of alternative ways to keep safe** in case the police do not respond right away.

Safety

☐ **Wait somewhere away from abuser** for police to arrive.

Inform (family, friends, neighbors, supervisor, human resource department, trusted coworkers, PAs/caregivers, and caseworkers) that you have a restraining order in effect and identify your abuser. You may wish to give some of these people a copy of the protection/restraining order.

Safety

SAFETY IN PUBLIC SETTINGS
(At school, on the job or at social, recreational or volunteer activities)

- **Decide who you will inform of your situation.** This could include your school, office or building security (provide a picture of your abuser if possible).

- Use an answering machine or another person to **screen your telephone calls**.

- **Devise a safety plan for when you are out in public.** Have someone escort you to your car, bus, taxi or other transportation. If possible, use a variety of routes to go home. Specialized vans routes are usually fixed so be prepared to work with the driver or others to plan for safety. Contact someone to let them know when you will arrive at your destination so they can check on your safe arrival. Think about what you would do if something happened while going to your destination.

- **Carry a cellular telephone programmed with 911.** 911 cannot trace the location of cellular telephones. If you cannot communicate your location, have someone assist you if possible.

- Ask your **workplace to discuss safety planning** with you and put a plan into place.

Asoral Publishing

Safety

• If you obtain a restraining order, ask the court to **order your abuser to not come to your workplace or school and to order your abuser to stay at least 500 feet away from you at all times.**

• Carry your restraining order with you and **give a copy to trustworthy people at your job, school or volunteer sites.**

• **Become familiar with the entrance and exits from any public building you frequent** so you know how to escape if necessary.

YOUR SAFETY & EMOTIONAL HEALTH

▪ If you are thinking of returning to or staying in a potentially abusive situation, **discuss an alternative plan** with someone you trust.

▪ **If you have to communicate or be with your abuser**, arrange to do so in a way that makes you feel safest, whether by telephone, writing a letter, e-mail or in the company of a third person. If you choose to see your abuser, protect yourself by doing so with a third party.

▪ **Have positive thoughts about yourself** and be assertive with others about your needs. Independent living centers, support groups and therapy can be helpful in building positive self-esteem and assertiveness skills.

▪ **Take care of your physical needs:** ask for assistance when needed.

▪ **Read or listen** to books, articles, music or poems that give you strength. The public library, independent living centers, and/or domestic violence programs may have these materials available in alternative forms.

▪ **Decide who you can call to talk freely and openly with**, and who can give you the support you need. Consider contacting a domestic violence hotline or having someone contact a

Safety

domestic violence hotline to strategize accessible support programs. Independent living centers and domestic violence shelters can work together to be more accommodating to safety and disability issues.

▪ Plan to **attend a womens' or victims' support group** for at least two weeks to gain support from others and learn more about yourself and your relationship. If a support group is physically inaccessible, ask for accommodations to be made. Also, work with your local independent living center to find supportive and knowledgeable counseling resources.

Safety

CONSIDER TAKING THE FOLLOWING ITEMS IF YOU LEAVE:

If you cannot take these items, have a copy of each paper item in your escape bag. However, remember that no item is more valuable then your safety.

Documentation
- Restraining or protection orders
- Driver's license or state I.D. card
- Birth certificates for you and your family members.
- Documents such as Social Security card, Social Security award letter, proof of disability, work permit, green card, passport
- Divorce and custody papers
- Lease, rental agreement, and/or house deed
- Car registration/car insurance papers
- Fixed route bus pass, mobility ID card, or special transit ID card

Financial
- Money, bank books, checkbooks, credit cards, ATM cards and mortgage payment book.
- Food stamps/AFDC Card

Medical
Insurance papers, Medicaid, Medical Assistance, clinic card, medical records, doctor's orders and prescriptions

Asoral Publishing

Safety

- Adaptive equipment (service animals, wheelchairs, shower bench, crutches, communication device, etc.)

- Medications, urological supplies, glasses, hearing aids, assistive devices needed for you and your children, grandchildren and dependents.

General Items

- Keys – house/car/office

- Personal items such as an address book, pictures (you, your children/grandchildren and your abuser), jewelry and items of sentimental value for you and your children/grandchildren

- Supplies for service animals

- Small, favorite toy of children/grandchildren who are leaving with you

- Toiletries/diapers

- Names and numbers of home health agencies, caseworkers and other disability service providers to assist in coordinating services for you

- Phone numbers of friends or past PAs/caregivers who might be willing to help

Safety

with personal care task during transitional period, and provide you with emotional support.

IMPORTANT TELEPHONE NUMBERS:
For information about domestic abuse services outside your community, call the following numbers:

National Domestic Violence Hotline at 1-800-799-SAFE (7233) or 1-800-787-3234 (TTY). For information on Full Faith and Credit:

Full Faith and Credit Project of the Pennsylvania Coalition Against Domestic Violence at 1-800-903-0111

For other information specific to abuse against individuals with disabilities contact:

National Council on Independent Living at 1-703-525-3406, 1-703-525-4153 (TTY)
Personal Safety Awareness Center at 1-512-385-5181, 1-512-482-0691 (TTY)
(Personal Safety for Individuals with Disabilities)
National Clearinghouse on Abuse in Later Life at 1-608-255-0539
Local Numbers:
Police _____
Domestic Abuse Program
_____
Adult Protective Services
_____

Asoral Publishing

Safety

Independent Living Center
_____

Aging Unit (Tribal or County)
_____

(if 60 or 65 – depending on state eligibility guidelines)
Health Care Provider
_____

Safety Tips for Victims of Domestic Violence

Tips to Share with a Victim to Plan for Safety

• **Tell** your kids that, if there's violence, their job is to stay safe, not to protect you. Find a safe place for them to stay in case of violence, such as with a neighbor or in a locked room. Teach them to call 911 and what to say to the dispatcher.

• **Hide** money, spare keys and a small bag of clothes at work or at a friend's house.

For small children, hide a favorite toy or stuffed animal that will comfort them.

• **Inform** your employer about the situation and develop a safety plan at work. Share a photo and description of the abuser with them and any pertinent legal documentation, such as a protection order.

• **Document** the abuse by taking photos of bruises and injuries, tell your doctor and get copies of your medical records; save threatening voicemails, notes and emails and write each incident down in a journal.

• **Gather** important documents or copies of documents such as passports, birth certificates, social security cards, insurance papers, work permits or green cards, ownership documents for car and/or house, checkbooks and bank account numbers. Hide these papers at work or at a friend's house. Know the abuser's social security number, birth date and place of birth.

• **Consider** obtaining a protection order. It directs the abuser not to contact, communicate with, attack, sexually assault or telephone you, your children or other family members. If you have a protection order, carry a copy of it with you at all times.

Safety Tips for Victims Planning on Staying – When You Are Afraid

• **Move** away from the kitchen, bathroom, garage or anyplace where there are dangerous sharp objects.

• **Plan** the easiest escape route. Decide on a door or window to exit quickly and safely. Make sure your kids know the route and practice it with them. Have a code word so they know when to call the law enforcement.

• **Don't** wear necklaces or scarves – these could be used to strangle you.

• **Always** make sure weapons are secured and that guns aren't loaded.

Safety Tips for Victims Who Have Left Their Abuser

• **Change** the locks on your doors. Install steel/metal doors, a security system, detectors and an outside lighting system.

• **Get** Caller ID for your telephone so you can screen your calls.

• **Consider** getting a post office box for your mail or participating in a confidential mailing program (if available in your state).

• **Learn** about your legal rights and options. If you have legal papers, keep copies of them with you at all times.

• **Tell** neighbors, friends, landlords or coworkers that your abusive partner no longer lives with you. Share your safety plan with people you trust. Explain it to your children.

• **Tell** your employer/coworkers about your situation and ask them to screen your calls, move your desk, change your work schedule/hours or accompany you to your car.

• **Tell** the school or day care or others spending time with your children who can pick them up and who can't. If you have a protective order, make sure they know about it.

• **Vary** your routes to work, to school or day care, to the grocery store and other places you frequent.

• **Call** a friend or someone else who will be supportive, when you feel down and ready to return to an abusive partner.

www.ingramcontent.com/pod-product-compliance
Lightning Source LLC
Chambersburg PA
CBHW060740050426
42449CB00008B/1276